The
Single-Parent
Family

The Single-Parent Family

LIVING HAPPILY IN A CHANGING WORLD

Marge Kennedy
and Janet Spencer King

CROWN TRADE PAPERBACKS   NEW YORK

To Caitlin, for being such a terrific kid.
M.K.
To Megan and Jamie, who mean everything to me.
J.S.K.

Copyright © 1994 by Marge Kennedy and Janet Spencer King

Published by Crown Publishers, Inc., 201 East 50th Street, New York, New York 10022. Member of the Crown Publishing Group. Random House, Inc. New York, Toronto, London, Sydney, Auckland

CROWN Trade Paperbacks™ and colophon are trademarks of Crown Publishers, Inc.

Manufactured in the United States of America

Library of Congress Cataloging-in-Publication Data

Kennedy, Marge M., 1950–
The single-parent family: living happily in a changing world / by Marge Kennedy and Janet Spencer King.—1st ed.
Includes bibliographical references and index.
1. Single-parent family—United States. 2. Child rearing—United States. 3. Parent and child—United States. 4. Parenting—United States. I. King, Janet Spencer. II. Title.
HQ777.4.K46 1994   93-13701
306.85'6—dc20   CIP

ISBN 0-517-88127-6

10 9 8 7 6 5 4 3 2 1

First Edition

Contents

Acknowledgments

Although a book may list one or, in our case, two authors, behind the names on the cover are many others—people who, through their willingness to share their professional insights and information, add immeasurably to the substance of a book; people who, through their willingness to share their feelings and experiences, add to its heart.

We have been fortunate in both areas to have found many people who showed great generosity toward us and our work in progress. In the professional world, we especially wish to thank the following: Linda Barbanel, M.S.W., C.S.W.; Sheila Berger, M.S.W., C.S.W.; Phyllis Diamond, M.S.W., C.S.W.; Earl Grollman, Ph.D.; Lucy H. Hedrick; Dorothy Jordon; Neil Kalter, Ph.D.; William H. Koch, M.D.; Lynn Leight, Ph.D.; Jane Mattes, M.S.W., C.S.W.; and Nancy Samalin, M.S. We also happily add to this list Irene Prokop, our editor at Crown, who gave us both professional insight and personal support, and Laura Farrell, whose enthusiastic research efforts made our job flow more smoothly. Our thanks, as well, to the staff at the Bank Street Bookstore.

The heart of our book comes from the hundreds of single parents we have met and talked with over the course of the last few years, and the many who filled out our extensive questionnaire. We heard from mothers and fathers in all parts of the country and from the whole range of socioeconomic strata. We were impressed by this group, with the obvious caring and commitment they have toward parenting in positive ways. A few of our single parents contributed extensive amounts of time and thought. A big thank you, then, to them: Ruth Adabody, Chris Economos, Sharon Guynup, Alan Hirshberg, Mary Mohler, Sharon Steen, Gary Yoshimura, Essie Wicks, and, also, to the members of Single Mothers by Choice.

Finally, we thank family and good friends for the love and caring they have heaped on us in generous amounts, as well as the encouragement they gave us as we made our way through seemingly endless amounts of research and writing. From Janet, special thanks to Alexa and Clair, Leland and Marti, and Carmen and Miriam for remembering that love really can conquer almost everything. Thanks also go to Bobbie and Lenny, Devra and Jose, Irene, Connie, Virginia and Ginny, Susan, and Mary for keeping the faith even when I wasn't so sure, and to Chris, who has never lost sight of his importance to the kids. From Marge, special thanks to Kathy and Tony, Kevin and Karen, Mary Ann and Tom, John, Laura, Michael, and Scott for giving Caitlin such a wonderfully diverse family to love. And to Kathleen, Ruth, Finola and Tom, Phyllis, Molly and Matt, Chris and Bill, Lauren and David, our friends from St. Paul's, and Donna, Vera, and the teachers of Columbia Greenhouse Nursery School, thanks for the kind of friendship that seems to know no bounds.

Introduction

Defining what makes a family is argued by leaders of government as well as television sitcom characters. All the debate, however, focuses on *who* the members are rather than *how* family members relate to one another. In truth, a family is what you make it. It is made strong, not by the number of heads counted at the dinner table, but by the rituals you help family members create, by the memories you share, by the commitment of time, caring, and love you show to one another, and by the hopes for the future you have as individuals and as a unit.

Single-parent families are as diverse—and as similar—as any other kind of family. We're large and small, demonstrative and reserved, neat and sloppy, even rich and maybe (sometimes!) broke. Perhaps we do suffer from something of an image problem—and that includes the issue of self-image—that our married counterparts don't face. We're asked, and sometimes left wondering ourselves, if one parent can really raise happy, healthy, and emotionally secure kids. (Let's face it: kids really could use six or seven parents on hand to fulfill their every need!)

For those of us who are doing this important job on our own, the time has come to look at who we really are and to find in ourselves and in the many well-functioning single-parent families around us a reason to be proud of the job we're doing.

In the real world—far removed from the doom-and-gloom preaching of politicians and the laugh-a-minute, make-believe world of TV and movies—single-parent homes are held together by ordinary moms or dads, most of whom care fiercely for their children, most of whom, in turn, are vibrant evidence that children raised in single-parent families can grow into happy, responsible, emotionally healthy adults.

The number of single-parent families in the U.S. is staggering. According to the 1990 Census, of the 35 million households in the United States with children under the age of eighteen, more than 10 million—close to one in three—are headed by single parents. Of these, 8.7 million households have single moms at the helm, and 1.4 million are headed by single dads. These single-parent families fall into four groups: single biological parents, single adoptive mothers and fathers, widows and widowers with children, and divorced parents.

There is strength in these numbers. It's not that parenting on our own gets any easier just because there are so many of us, but it's encouraging to know that so many in this group are functioning extremely well, as parents, as children, as families, as models for us all.

Anyone living through the experience knows that the waters of single parenthood aren't without dangerous rapids and murky depths. But there are many ways to navigate a successful course— which includes keeping the ship intact during the inevitable storms. In the pages that follow, we investigate the real world of families living in single-parent homes. We examine what single parents can do to contribute to their own and their children's emotional well-being and what factors make a happy childhood possible for our kids now and a happy adulthood likely in their futures.

As a sort of sneak preview, we'll tell you right here what is the single biggest determinant of your kids' chances for a richly fulfilling life: *You.* Research shows over and over again that the presence of one stable, loving parent who is willing to give her or his children the time, attention, and care they need is *the* major factor in creating a happy outcome.

Every single parent shares some very fundamental fears and hopes: Will I be a good enough parent? Will my children grow into the kinds of adults I hope they will be? Will there be enough time between inevitable crises to create joyous times and happy memories for my kids? Because we, the authors, are single parents—one of us through divorce and one of us through an unmarried and unplanned but happily accepted pregnancy—we found ourselves often turning to experts for advice about child raising. Although we uncovered tomes of good information about raising kids, we found that the specific needs of children being raised in one-parent homes were generally relegated to end-of-book afterthoughts, usually under such headings as "Special Problems of Single Parents."

Well, there's more to single parenthood than special problems. There are also special joys, special commitments, special moments on which to build a firm and a happy future. When we turned to books designed especially for single parents, we found to our chagrin that they, too, focused far more on getting through our children's childhoods, rather than celebrating these precious years with them.

We believe that living in our kind of family is not a substitute life, not a holding pattern, but a full one. Out of this belief—that our families are indeed whole—came this book. We hope that it proves as helpful to you who read it as it was to us in researching and writing it.

1

Taking Care
of You

In the lives of most single parents, there is a lot of caretaking. Single parents take care of their kids, their homes, their work, their finances, their yard, and their pets. It's ironic, then, that so many single parents overlook taking care of the one person who is holding the kids, the home, the job, the finances, the yard, and the pets together—you.

The list of reasons single parents can give you about why they don't take such good care of themselves is generally a long one and, on the surface, a reasonable one: There's not enough time, not enough energy, the kids' needs are pressing, there's always work to be done. "My day starts at six-fifteen when the alarm rings, and I'm off and running," says a single mother of three in Minneapolis. "It ends at night after I've put the kids in bed, straightened up the house, and looked over my notes for my next day's meetings at work; by then I'm ready to fall exhausted into my bed. As far as I'm concerned, taking care of me is just a big 'should' in my life, and I have too many of those already."

This mother's attitude is understandable, but her viewpoint, like that of so many single parents, reflects a misunderstanding of both the importance of self-care and what self-care actually is.

REPLENISHING YOURSELF

When you spend some of your valuable time and energy on yourself, you are, in essence, filling your personal-resource bank. Life makes harsh and constant demands of everyone, none more so than of a single mom or dad. Constantly giving means that you've got to be sure there's something going back in as well, or you'll risk becoming emotionally short-changed, if not actually bankrupt. The acts of doing for yourself, the kindnesses, pleasures, and understanding you offer yourself, are the deposits you place in your personal-resource account. They are the reserves you can draw on when your personal strength begins to ebb.

Learning to place your own well-being on your "to-do" list may require some rethinking on your part. If, right now, you're saying to yourself, "Sure, as soon as I take care of the umpteen other things on my list, I really will take a moment for me," remember this: Your ability to take care of others rests largely on how well you're feeling. Remind yourself, as well, that you're a person too and you deserve a rewarding life just as much as your kids, your boss, your friends, co-workers, or anyone else. It's true, of course, that there probably isn't another person around nudging you to find your own life pleasures or reminding you that you have a right to them. You'll have to be your personal cheerleader in this, but don't let your sole voice be overwhelmed by the clamor of others.

If you still need convincing, consider, then, the following scenario: "It's Saturday after a hard work week. You've finished the laundry and squeezed in attending the Junior League soccer game. The house needs a cleaning and your preteen daughter is having two friends spend the night (must pick up microwave popcorn and ice cream). You have a couple of hours open in your schedule this afternoon in which you could (a) take the car in for an oil change and emissions test, (b) go to the gym for a workout and a short swim followed by a cup of European coffee at the corner coffee house, or (c) clean the house." Now, picture yourself having done (a). Good for you, you took care of the car. Or maybe you chose (c). Later on, as the kids have spread the sofa cushions through the living room, and popcorn kernels are strewn all over the carpet, you may curb your frustration long enough to wonder why you spent your time and energy making the house look great when no one cared but you. But now picture yourself having chosen *(b)*. You're glowing from an invigorating workout and a swim in water that was just the right temperature. The coffee was fresh and you read your new novel for thirty minutes without interruption. Will you find supervising three lively little girls for the night less tiresome, maybe even fun, having just come from taking care of the car or the house—or from taking care of you?

Taking care of yourself is obviously much broader than how you spend your Saturday afternoons. Maximizing your well-being involves not only what you do for yourself but also understanding your emotional state (and, if necessary, changing it), your stress factors, and the ease with which you conduct your daily life. However, reduced to its simplest terms, taking care of yourself means validating and meeting your own needs. Naturally, the specifics are going to be at least a little different for everyone, but there are aspects of self-care that hold true for all.

Giving Yourself Psychic Space

The first part of self-care that holds true for everyone is the need to give yourself psychic space. No, the term *psychic space* isn't New Age babble. Psychic space means having the opportunity to be who you are, not Justin's mother or Sara's father, not an employee of the Jolly Pie Company or a law partner in a Wall Street firm, not the PTA volunteer or the Little League assistant. Psychic space is the chance to be you, with none of your numerous labels attached. In your own psychic space there is only you—the person who may enjoy modern detective stories and medieval art, the person who may like working into the night and sleeping into the day, the person who may love crowded parties but have only one best friend.

Creating your psychic space isn't an outwardly dramatic act, and it can usually be easily slipped into your day. You may satisfy the need through your choice of reading during your workday commute, whether it be thrillers or inspirational self-help. One single mother of three young boys, who almost never has a moment on her own, gets her psychic space through twice-weekly aerobics classes. "People think I do this because the exercise is so energizing," she says, laughing. "That's true, and I do love it, but the real reason I like going to class so much is something else. Not many people know this, because I rarely show it, but the fact is that I am very competitive. I get huge satisfaction from looking around that class and reaffirming that I am the best one there. Maybe I shouldn't admit being so competitive, but there it is, and my aerobics let me satisfy the need."

A single dad in suburban New York finds his self-nurturing at his once-monthly poetry workshop, where for a few hours he is neither dad, the telephone repairman, nor the part-time carpenter. "I find that, whatever else I'm doing, I'm always saving mental notes for the workshop. It's a creative outlet that I just don't have anyplace else in my life."

Giving Yourself the Gift of Time

A second aspect of taking care of yourself is granting yourself the time to be who you are. Time, of course, is the one life commodity that most single parents can lay little claim to, since the segments of single parents' days are generally attached to others and other responsibilities. Fortunately, time for yourself doesn't have to be a lot of time. It does, however, require that you allot yourself a set number of minutes or hours on a regular basis.

One New York single mother of a preschool girl says that she is "embarrassingly content" with her life, and, in spite of chronic money worries, seldom feels in any way trapped or overwhelmed, as some of her other single-mother friends report. "I'm very happy working and taking care of my daughter," she says: I have a lot of responsibility, but I don't usually feel at all put upon. That is, as long as I have my morning time. You see, I love the newspaper, and as long as I get a chance to read it without interruption, I can deal with everything else. To be sure I get that chance, I drop my daughter off at her nursery school fifteen minutes early. Then before getting to work, I go to the corner coffee shop, where I read my paper, uninterrupted by anyone or anything, for fifteen minutes. It's truly a ritual for me, and if I miss it I have no patience the rest of the day.

You may find that granting yourself even a small measure of time each day cuts into other scheduled tasks. But time for yourself is so important that it's worth a bit of compromise. Many single parents, for instance, find the time they need to get in touch with themselves at night, during a wind-down period alone before going to bed. Your having this chance, however, is not necessarily something your kids will easily accommodate. "My kids are the worst when it comes to bedtime," reports a single dad in Dallas. "They keep popping up to tell me one more thing, long after I've put them to bed. I have to have an hour or so completely to myself at night or I feel unsettled, and I don't consider it my time until the kids are actually asleep. So I just hang in there until the kids have finally dozed off. I've been known to stay up well past midnight on work nights, just to give myself that hour."

A Luxury a Day

Luxury may seem far removed from the reality of any parent's life. But not only should you as a single parent have luxury, you should have a sampling of it each and every day. The reality check here, though, is the nature of the luxuries you choose. If you give it some thought, you'll probably discover you have a range of small pleasures you enjoy. These might include a long hot bath with music in the background, jogging, fresh flowers on your table, or clean, fresh sheets on your bed. One divorced single mother with her own business has a set routine for Wednesday nights, the evening her two young children are with their dad. "I pick my sheets up from the laundry that night, rent myself a video, and make myself some popcorn. Then I hop into my freshly made bed and luxuriate in the feel of the sheets, the movie, and the quiet in my home. I find it incredibly calming," she says.

Naturally, there are days when there's no time for a run, a long bath, or a night in bed watching a movie. But you can always squeeze in some luxury for yourself each day, even a small one. Maybe some smoked salmon or a specialty cheese that you buy just for you (no need to feel guilty, if you keep in mind all the cookies you buy for the kids); maybe reading a magazine or calling a friend after dinner. There's always something nice in the offing, if you look for it. The secret is to get in the habit of being good to yourself, even in small doses.

Connecting to Friends

One of the most important of all ways to replenish yourself is maintaining relationships with friends. Friends are not luxuries; they are necessities. Interacting with other adults brings a certain balance that can go askew when it's just you and the kids. Friends help restore your sense of humor; they can share in the amusement of children's foibles and the ironies of family life. Friends renew your confidence; they believe in you and recognize your strengths, including the times when you've lost faith in both. Friends offer you their strength, someone to lean on when you feel you're being overwhelmed by all those leaning on you. Friends bring you companionship and caring.

Because you are a single parent, it's through your friendships that you fill a need that is almost as intense and as ongoing as your need for food. That is the need all parents have to discuss their kids—the good about them, the bad about them, and even the ugly. In a functional two-parent family, parents fill this need through each other. Single parents, without a close relationship with the other parent, need to have someone else with whom they can share the parent side of themselves. Some single parents slip into a comfortable ongoing dialogue about their kids with one or two good friends or relatives. Others find they must establish the dialogue more consciously, generally with a new friend who is in a similar situation. "My sister moved across the country," says a single mother in Washington, D.C.: "Her move left me without anyone to report my kids' activities and problems to. Since she was a daily part of my life, I didn't feel guilty bragging or complaining about my children. She never thinks I am obnoxious or that the kids are horrible brats when I vent my anxiety and frustration about them, because she sees the whole picture. After her move I started spending more time with a co-worker who is a bit older than I am and whose kids are now in college. In the last few months, we have developed a set routine. I come in, we each get a cup of coffee, and we discuss how things are going with our kids. I don't always take her advice, but it's generally pretty sound. And she is always happy to listen. I am especially grateful for that."

Before you confide your private feelings about your children—whether it is your pride in their accomplishments or your despair in their mistakes—be sure your proposed confidante is someone who is trustworthy and nonjudgmental. In the best of all worlds, the person to whom you reveal your innermost thoughts about the people you hold most dear also shares your outlook on raising kids and cares about your children personally. These continuing conversations with a parenting confidante can offer you incalculable comfort and support.

Good friends don't require a great deal of time. With friends, you know you're there for each other without daily reminders. But good friends do call for regular checking-in, and, of course, you must be willing to give back in return. At times you may feel that it's tough to give back, because all the places in your life are filled by your kids. If that's the case, find or make room for friends, too. You won't regret it.

Sharing Your Sense of Self with the Kids

It may surprise you to hear this, but your kids probably know little about you. To them you're mom. Or dad. They see you as their caretaker almost exclusively, and they're undoubtedly quite happy about your circumscribed role. This can, however, become problematic for you. Since the kids are the people with whom you spend the most time, you too might start seeing yourself mostly in the somewhat pallid and homogenized caregiver mode, losing sight of the unique blend of characteristics and the endearing quirks that make you distinctive from all others. There's much to be said for letting the kids in on who you really are.

There's no need to share your autobiography. You can help your kids get to know the real you in the course of a normal day. The next time you're watching a TV sitcom together, for instance, tell them why you find something particularly funny. When you go to the movies, explain what it is about certain types of stories and particular actors that you like or dislike. Muster up some gusto for your favorite foods (although you probably shouldn't talk about foods you don't like, or your kids may never eat them again). Don't be shy about establishing your birthday and special days as important events. "A few weeks before my birthday or Christmas," says a single mother in Boston, "I lasso my son into doing some chores or errands, for which I pay him. I'm completely upfront about the fact that this money is for my gift. Then I arrange with a friend to take him out to find an appropriate present for me. She is one of his favorite grown-ups, so they always have fun shopping together. I feel it's important for my son to realize that I'm supposed to be on the receiving end of things now and then." If your children are very young, you can also recruit a relative or close friend to conspire with them about a gift for you and a method of celebrating. Should you get a promotion or raise, take everyone for a festive dinner and let the kids know the reason for your celebration. You'll be teaching the kids that it is important to celebrate not only you, but all people whom they love, and you'll be reminding them that you're worthy of receiving good things, too.

MAKING YOUR LIFE EASIER

It's often said that it's not so much what happens to a person but how he or she handles it that determines its effect. Single parents have a lot happening on most days, which may not usually cause problems. But when there is chronically too much stress and too little time, the demands of life may start to feel overwhelming. Consequently, learning to diminish stress and to maximize available time offers the potential for more comfortable living.

The Challenge of Stress

Stress is frequently looked at as the scourge of the modern-day world. The fact is, though, that stress is just part of living and, because it is energy-producing, it can be a positive aspect of your life. Stress developed its bad reputation because so many people allow it to get out of hand. The challenge, then, is not to rid your life of stress but to learn more about managing it. The goal is to put you in charge of stress instead of the other way around.

As a single parent, you probably have more than your share of anxiety. It's particularly important for you to understand what may be causing you undue amounts of pressure and how you may be able to minimize either negative stress itself or the effects of it.

Stress in Single-Parent Homes

High stress isn't good for anyone, but high stress in single-parent homes can have particularly negative consequences. A 1991 study conducted at Temple University highlighted single-parent families in which the mothers (the focus of this study) were overly stressed. The authors of the study, Marcy Gringlas and Marsha Weinraub, report that they found no behavioral differences among children raised by single mothers for whom stress was low and those kids raised in two-parent homes. Additionally, the children of single moms were not disturbed by occasional periods of stress; rather, it was when high stress existed in the home over an extended period of time that the children became troubled. Chronic maternal stress in these homes resulted in preadolescents who showed increased anxiety, inattentiveness at school, and depression.

Don't immediately assume, if you're among the stressed, that this study gives you something else to add to your guilt list. In fact, the study reinforces that, although many single mothers were stressed, most were just as responsive to their kids and as warm as any of the married mothers studied. So don't let the study increase your stress levels, but use it to underline how important it is for you and your kids to keep stress in check.

Stress-Management Techniques

The most effective technique for stress management, of course, is to reduce the kind that debilitates you. (For many single parents, the biggest cause of stress is money; we discuss that fully in Chapter 4.) An excellent way to start your own stress-reduction program is by taking control of your emotional state. First, recognize that there's nothing inherently wrong with you for feeling overwhelmed at times—raising kids on your own is stressful. Then consider the circumstances that brought you to single parenthood and the impact that may be having on your life. If you are a single parent by choice, having given birth or adopted without a spouse, you may spend much of your time luxuriating in your new role. Nevertheless, sleep deprivation and the anxiety that comes with new parenthood are bound to take their toll. If you come to single parenthood through divorce (as more than eighty percent do) or widowhood, you should have a careful look at yourself to evaluate any lingering emotional fallout.

Virtually all those who are widowed and many who have divorced, as well as their children, experience grief to a greater or lesser extent. Familiarize yourself with the pattern of grief, which generally includes these four stages: *Denial,* the inability to believe this event has happened to you, is the earliest stage of grief and the one most people quickly pass through. *Anger* is second, and it is here that many people get stuck as the anger hangs on (more about anger in Chapter 3). The third stage is *despair,* in which your belief in having a better life—ever—seems unlikely. Finally comes *acceptance,* the phase in which the mourner becomes able to get back into the mainstream of living.

If any of the first three stages of grief seem to be dogging you, take action. Support groups, particularly, can give you real insight and both greater self-awareness and healing. Just having the company and comfort of others who have walked the same path can make coping more manageable. Additionally, there are numerous helpful books on the subjects of divorce and widowhood and their emotional impact.

Depression is another debilitating condition that many who go through major life upheavals have to combat. Everyone has bad days, especially those making adjustments to new ways of living. But if you find the melancholy feelings starting to overwhelm you, if you are chronically listless and find little in life to cheer you up, look into getting professional help. Low-cost support is available through a number of different services. Ask your friends who have been in therapy for suggestions, or call your doctor. Many of the religious-affiliated clinics, such as Catholic or Jewish Family Services, have sliding-scale therapy fees. You can also call the psychiatric division of a teaching hospital in your area for references to clinics.

Even if you haven't yet found your emotional equilibrium, you can still incorporate some of the following stress-management techniques into your life. You'll be surprised how much you can alter the dynamics that once led you to being chronically stressed. None of the techniques described here is particularly difficult; indeed, some are disarmingly simple. But when put into practice, they can go far to help you relax the knot in your stomach and ease those persistent headaches.

Anticipate the Unexpected. Without a backup, single parents are more stressed by the unexpected but inevitable last-minute changes in plans and routines. The common situation of waking up to a child who is too sick to go to school or to the child-care center can throw any parent into turmoil. Other typical stress-making scenarios including discovering, as you're walking out the door, that today's a half day at school, that you suddenly have to work late, or that, waking up one morning, *you're* the one who is too sick to get up and take care of the kids. While these are emergencies at the moment, they are predictable, in that all do occur on occasion. Develop a plan of action ahead of time for each of these or other likely scenarios that would make your stress levels soar. Have a list of baby-sitters who are free during the day.

Make prearrangements with an at-home parent to cover any half days by taking your child home, and return the favor by taking her child for part of the weekend. Develop a buddy system at the child-care center for another parent to take your child home when you have a late-night work crisis. Keep your food pantry well stocked so that you don't have to go to the market with the flu, and have some favorite videos on hand to entertain the children. Good friends are your allies at times like these; don't be reluctant to call if you need extra provisions while you're sick in bed or if you need someone to take your kids for a few hours.

Review Your Expectations—of Yourself, Your Kids, and Your Life. Unrealistic expectations are major sources of stress, whether of yourself, your kids, or life in general. Take some time to review all your broad expectations. Refining them may save you untold amounts of stress. For example, if a messy house unravels your nerves, it may be time to adjust your standards to meet the reality of young kids on the premises. Perhaps by simplifying your dinner menus you can also save some time and energy.

Kids on TV or in literature may always behave in a seemly fashion, but yours probably don't. No real kid does all the time. Naturally your children should be reasonably well behaved, but there is nothing to be gained for any of you by being too demanding about the little stuff. Before you make a demand of your children, ask yourself if it's *really* important. If not, give the kids the benefit of being themselves and not replicas of what others define as "perfect."

In the same vein, are you asking too much of yourself? Remember, the best parent is "the good enough parent." This belief is held by many experts, including the late child-development professor Bruno Bettleheim, who used the expression as the title for his last book.

Give Yourself Reminders Every Day That You're Doing the Best Job You Can. A pat on the back, even when administered by your own hand, offsets the stress that builds up from that critical internal voice. Be your own best friend, and counter the critic inside you with well-deserved compliments.

Learn How and When to Give Yourself Rewards. Organization expert Lucy Hedrick, herself a single mother and the author of *Five Days to an Organized Life,* has a lot to say about stress reduction. She identifies four key components of stress reduction: proper exercise, proper nutrition, enough sleep, and time management (more on time management follows). Hedrick, who teaches organization in workshops, reports that nearly every single parent she has met feels guilty about taking time for himself or herself. "It's true across the board," she reports. Consequently, she has devised a system specifically to get people to open up time blocks for themselves and to use this time for personal satisfaction. Her system revolves around learning how to give yourself rewards.

Surprisingly, when faced with a reward possibility, many people can't think of a thing to do. Hedrick suggests you keep a pocket notebook with you at all times and start a list of rewards that might interest you. Write down activities as you think of them, anything that crosses your mind as something you'd like to do, from window shopping at the mall to spending a day in a museum. Hedrick then suggests you note the time frames for your reward entries, say ten minutes for tea to two hours for a hair appointment. To incorporate these into daily life, Hedrick has her clients tie them to the completion of chores. Before you start the laundry or the annual report for your department at work, decide what reward you will give yourself upon finishing. The laundry may rate only ten minutes for reading the paper, while the report may earn you dinner out with a friend. At first you may find it as difficult to act on your rewards as it is to get your kids to eat enough veggies. You may also have to moderate your reward list because of financial or time restraints. Although these daily rewards seem pale when compared to your long-term goals, they are the treats you can have now—you've earned them.

Seek Inner Peace. Many people find inner quiet that ultimately exudes into their daily life through prayer or taking time each day for quiet reflection. Some find meditation amazingly helpful in containing stress. You don't need a guru or an expensive course to learn the basics of effective meditation. Any number of books can give you those. The time-out from stress that reflective practices offer helps quiet the need to be in control of all situations as well. Whether you turn to a higher power or seek your spiritual core within yourself, stepping outside the merely physical realm puts the world in a new and freeing perspective.

Managing Your Time

Time is one of life's great equalizers. Rich or poor, everyone has the same twenty-four hours a day. Since you probably have more to accomplish in that twenty-four hours than many others, you'll no doubt want to use your time as efficiently as possible. While you may rightly feel that there are never enough hours to do everything you need to do, you can take heart that, as a single parent, you have a small bonus when it comes to time. A study by John P. Robinson at the University of Maryland reports that single parents actually have several *more* leisure hours per week than their married counterparts. This is not to say that any parent has enough hours, but it's clear that spouses take time.

Even so, single parents often find themselves rushing the normal tempo of life. Too fast a pace leaves you worn out at the end of the day, usually with errands undone because you're too tired to do them. Learning to manage your time better allows you to get more done, makes for a more peaceful environment, and gives you a greater sense of personal control, which goes far in helping reduce stress.

To help organize personal-time management, start with the following:

Don't Spend Energy Worrying About What You're Not Getting Done. Ms. Hedrick, who also authored *365 Ways to Save Time,* identifies chronic anxiety about getting things done as one of the greatest time thiefs. She dubs it "to-do-itis." Instead of concentrating on how much you have to do, focus your energy on how to go about setting up a smoother schedule for yourself.

Get Yourself Time-Management Tools. Hedrick recommends two invaluable purchases: a pocket notebook and a pocket calendar. Keep both with you at all times so that you never have to waste time looking for them. In the notebook, record all the minutiae you need to tend to—errands to run, things to pick up, reminders to yourself and others. This not only serves as a working list, the pocket-notebook technique also frees you from having to think about the pesky details of life until it's actually time to take care of a given task. The pocket calendar works in much the same way. You might want to transfer some dates to a large family calendar at home, but an up-to-date calendar in your pocket means your schedule is literally at your fingertips at all time.

Prioritize Your Tasks. This time-honored technique is popular because it works. The idea, of course, is to sort out your to-do list, and then divide the items into those you must do and those you can put off for a rainy Sunday someday. You can streamline your schedule by advance planning, too, such as doing the loop to the drugstore, the dry cleaners, the stationery store, and the supermarket all at once, instead of running out again and again. In a similar vein, if you're headed someplace and can tack an errand onto it, do so and cross one more item off your list.

Match Your Energy Levels to the Required Work. You can make doing your daily tasks easier and faster by slotting them into the times *you*—night owl or morning lark—are most up for the chore. For instance, you might find clearing the dishwasher truly tiresome at night but a breeze in the morning. It only makes sense, then, to do chores that allow you to sit and perhaps watch TV in the evening, and to save more physically demanding ones (even putting away dishes) for the morning, when you can zip through them.

Get Up Fifteen Minutes Earlier in the Morning. Forcing yourself out of bed will make you unhappy only for a few minutes. Giving yourself the bonus of an extra fifteen minutes a day will mean an unharried start that will make the whole day better for you and your family.

TEN TIME-SAVERS

1. Make stews and other one-pot meals to cut down on cleanup and to have dinners readily available throughout the week. Train each child to carry his or her plate and one other item back to the sink or refrigerator after each meal.

2. Choose clothes and pack backpacks and briefcases the night before to avoid being rushed in the morning. Put everything that you and your kids need to take to school or work the next morning by the door before you go to bed.

3. Bathe younger children together. If your children are young enough to need supervision while they bathe, clean the bathroom, do any hand laundry, or catch up on reading while they play in the tub. Or use bath time as a special playtime and conversation time for you and your young children.

4. If you can stand it, let kids sleep in sweat suits that they can wear out the next morning to avoid hassles about getting dressed. Or at least make sure the kids are in clean underwear and socks before they go to bed.

5. Do an extra fifteen minutes of housekeeping every night to help free up weekends for more playful activity.

6. Get rid of anything around the house that you're not using but nevertheless move, dust, or devote any other time to.

7. Store toys and clothes in large baskets or boxes to make cleanup and access easier. Use smaller baskets to stash hair clips and so forth. Keep another basket readily available for dropping in game pieces and other items that didn't get put away the first time, so you can find them when you want them.

8. Cut down on paperwork. Pay bills as they come in; pay as many bills as possible by automatic-payroll or bank-account deductions. Order stamps by mail. Buy a

box of greeting cards to use as needed, rather than running out each time you need one. Keep a file of important documents in order to save having to look for them, or worse, having to replace them if lost.

9. Shop with a list in order to cut down on frequent, often unnecessary, trips. Have goods delivered when possible, rather than hauling everything home yourself.

10. Ignore what you can.

PROFESSIONAL POINT OF VIEW

JANE MATTES, M.S.W., C.S.W., founder of Single Mothers by Choice, a support organization for mothers who have chosen or are considering single parenthood, and author of *Single Mothers by Choice.*

Q. Becoming a single parent of an infant certainly comes with its own stresses. What's the most important thing that single parents of newborns need to do to make the transition to single parenthood less unnerving?

A. Find a support system. When a parent is married, the entire support system exists in the spouse. When alone with a baby, you need to have several people filling the various roles. No one person is able to replace a spouse. Look for friends to help you out in practical ways, friends to just listen, friends to be an adult and not just a parent with. Of course, I also really believe it's helpful to be part of a support group, which provides you with resources of people and advice from outside your immediate circle.

Q. Being so involved in the lives of children can leave single parents little time or energy for themselves. How can single parents best meet their own needs for nurturance?

A. The first and most important thing is to acknowledge having your own needs. Realize, too, that meeting your own needs makes you a more satisfied parent. It's not a selfish act to take care of yourself. In fact, you're failing your child if you fail yourself. Don't lose sight of the fact that your own needs are sometimes different from your child's needs. An infant needs you almost one hundred percent, so your own needs will have to take a back seat to your child's at that point in his or her life. Your ability to take care of yourself increases in proportion to your child's age. A ten year old can handle—can benefit from—knowing you have a life separate from his.

Q. Many single parents are quite content in the intense one-on-one relationship they have with their children. Can there be too much intensity?
A. The key word is *balance*. Of course, every parent-and-child relationship is intense. But your child should not be your only source of gratification. Your child can't be your friend, your confidante, the only person with whom you feel physical closeness. Single parents, if we're not careful, can look for inappropriate gratification from our children. But our kids are not here to comfort us, to entertain us, or to validate us. Those things need to come from ourselves and from other adults.

Q. All parents have to learn to let go a little as children grow up. Are there any special considerations for single parents facing this issue?
A. Kids who live with two loving parents can turn from one to the other as they need to. If Mom's being a grouch, there's always Dad to offer a safe haven. Kids of single parents need a safe haven, too. So it's really important for a child to be encouraged to love others and not just you. Our relationship with our children is so one-on-one that we may have to make a real effort to allow them to experience intimacy with others. Every kid needs to know that love comes delivered in different packages. Knowing that they're loved by others and can love others is emotionally fortifying under any circumstances, but it's particularly important at those times when you've locked horns with your kids. Then, especially, they need to know there's someone else to go to. You're giving a child a gift when you give him someone else to love.

Q. Are there any practical suggestions that you've heard from single parents about making the nuts and bolts of our lives easier?
A. Keep expectations to the lowest possible minimum. A day without wanting to run screaming from the room is a plus. Everything else is gravy. Seriously, it just comes down to being kind to yourself, letting the small stuff with the kids slide, and congratulating one and all on getting through each day relatively well. We've all got to remember to pick our battles carefully, to be prepared to lose small ones, and to hold out for big ones. Years from now, it won't really matter if your kid left his socks on the floor for the tenth time this week. What will matter is how safe and secure a child feels growing up. Remember: Kids don't care if your house is clean. The more of the little annoyances you can learn to live with, the better off you'll all be. Save your strength for the things that matter.

Q. In the years since you founded Single Mothers by Choice, what differences, if any, have you noticed in society's response to single parenthood?
A. I think the biggest change is that people now understand that there are different types of single parents. Single mothers, particularly, are no longer lumped into one category. We're no longer assumed to be unwed teens or deserted women. It's clear to more and more people that we include mature, strong people with jobs, independence, and a sense of self. So many of us have more experience with life. We are capable of providing the practical and emotional support that once seemed out of the realm of single parenthood. There's now an acknowledgment that the issues of single parenthood are different for us than the issues faced by single parents of a generation ago. Our concerns are more likely to be the concerns of all parents. Our kids are not so set apart. They're not pitied. There's also the recognition, which we sometimes deny even to ourselves, that in some ways our lives are actually easier than the lives of married parents. A spouse takes a lot of energy.

2

Establishing the Foundation for Family Life

W e were all tired and hungry and, as usual, the kids were picking on each other," recalls a single mother of two from Chicago. I asked my son to do something—I don't even remember what—and he balked. My daughter, who was thirteen at the time, then stunned me by telling her brother, 'Leave Mom alone. She's a single mother and she's doing the best she can.' I thought, What has happened here that she sees me as a victim and our family as somehow very different from other families?"

Yes, single-parent families are different from two-parent families. And urban families are different from rural ones, and families with six kids and a dog are different from one-child, no-pet households. But even if there is only one adult presiding at the dinner table, yours is every bit as much a real family as are the Waltons. Keeping that sense of yourself and your kids as a living, loving, growing entity firmly in your mind is the foundation of your family's life, and its importance can not be overstated.

In the early years of single parenthood, you are putting into place the habits, routines, and the sense of identity of your new household. You are establishing how family members relate to you and to one another. These years are unquestionably full of challenge, but there can be great satisfaction, too, as you begin to see the benefits of your hard work pay off for your family. As you get out from under the initial adjustment to single parenthood and move on to the rhythms of raising a family, it helps not only to visualize your future but to be able to visualize the various configurations that make up families and to see how each of these affect how members relate to one another.

UNDERSTANDING FAMILY DYNAMICS

Back in the 1950s, traditional two-parent/two-child families were deemed "square" in the lingo of the anti-Establishment. Little did they know that decades later the Establishment would almost come to agree with this assessment. Over the years, family-systems therapists have developed a visual aid to help family members better understand how differing family structures affect relationships. Indeed, these graphic devises show the two-parent/two-children unit in the form of a square (see diagrams on next page). In this structure, there are twelve lines of relationship:

1) from husband to wife;
2) from wife to husband;
3) from father to child 1;
4) from father to child 2;
5) from mother to child 1;
6) from mother to child 2;
7) from child 1 to mother;
8) from child 2 to mother;
9) from child 1 to father;
10) from child 2 to father;
11) from child 1 to child 2; and
12) from child 2 to child 1.

In a one-parent/two-child home (a triangle), the number of daily, routine-producing relationships is reduced, not by one, but by half:

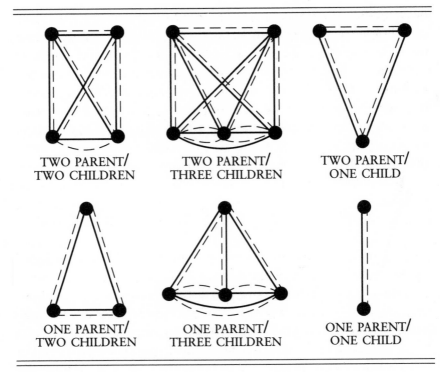

TWO PARENT/
TWO CHILDREN

TWO PARENT/
THREE CHILDREN

TWO PARENT/
ONE CHILD

ONE PARENT/
TWO CHILDREN

ONE PARENT/
THREE CHILDREN

ONE PARENT/
ONE CHILD

1) parent to child 1;
2) parent to child 2;
3) child 1 to parent;
4) child 2 to parent;
5) child 1 to child 2; and
6) child 2 to child 1.

While the number of relationships is reduced, the intensity of the relationship of children to parent is increased, since they merge on just one point—you. The intensity of one-parent/one-child families is even greater, as shown in the straight-line configuration, because each member focuses his or her attention on the other.

Whether a family forms a square, triangle, or straight line is not a judgmental issue. "There is nothing wrong with any of these," notes Sheila Berger, M.S.W.,C.S.W, a family-systems therapist practicing in New York City. "Families in square, triangular, or single-line configurations can function equally well, but they cannot function in the same ways." Berger goes on to point out that problems erupt when the family changes but family members continue to carry the expectations of the old family structure and act as if it still exists. It's similar to thinking that having a new baby won't change the way your family operates. On the other hand, those who expect that many, many things will change when a person joins or leaves a family are in a far better position to react appropriately.

A Seattle mother of a son and daughter recalls becoming extremely (and uncharacteristically) short tempered with her kids shortly after her husband moved out. She had wanted the separation and had expected her children's hurt to counter her own feelings of relief. She had also been prepared to feel a bit overwhelmed by the additional responsibility. But what she hadn't counted on was the new intensity of her kids' need for her, both practically and emotionally. Nor had she realized that with only herself and her kids in the house, and no spouse on which to focus her everyday annoyances or to turn to for help on occasion, she too shifted a much greater degree of attention on the children. She had assumed her short temper with her kids would ease as she and they became used to the separation. But as time went on, she felt she was becoming, if anything, more ferocious. Then, about two years into single parenthood, she hired a college student to live with them to help out with child care and housework. "I was astonished at the difference it made in me," she says. "My good humor with the kids returned, and our fights decreased in number and in pitch. Suddenly, we had a relatively calm household again." Bringing another responsible adult into the picture, she realized, defused the chronic pressure she was under and gave her children another person with whom they could relate. In effect, she restructured her triangular family into a square.

While not every family can reconfigure itself in this way, every family can benefit from learning to rethink the family structure and openly acknowledging the changed dynamics. Family-systems therapists refer to this kind of rethinking as "reframing." Reframing allows each person to recognize that attitudes and behaviors naturally change when the family structure changes, and that what is abnormal in a two-parent family might be normal in a one-parent home. For example, many children in single-parent homes worry a great deal about the well-being of their custodial parents. Berger explains, "In a two-parent family, this kind of excessive concern could be considered neurotic. However, in the case of a single-parent home, the child is correct in recognizing the critical role this one person plays in his life. It's only normal, then, for him to worry a great deal about this parent's continued safety."

An example of this reframing comes from a Connecticut mother of a nine-year-old son, who recalls changes in her son's behavior after her divorce. "After our divorce, our son, Justin, started demanding to know where I'm going, who I'm with, when I'll be home. If I'm more than a few mintues late, he's frantic." To deal with her son's new behavior, this mother had to do some serious evaluating of the situation and her reactions to it. "I really resented it at first. It made me feel sort of trapped. But I started to look at it from Justin's point of view and began to understand how scary it must be for him not to know where I am and if I'm okay. I've learned to be sure that he never has to worry about me. I've had to go looking for a phone at some pretty awkward times, but I always call, no matter what, if I'm going to be late getting home."

Recognizing Your Many Roles

Single parents enjoy all the pleasures—and endure all the pains—of parenthood and then some. For those who were previously married, your spouse may have done a portion of the housework, taken care of bill paying, or supervised the kids' homework. But these are now all your jobs, along with the roles you had before. You may also be working outside the home for the first time in a long time. As a single parent, you're forced to juggle schedules, fatigue, child care, and finances in a whole new way. Don't think for a minute that you have to (or can) do it all perfectly. The only really important things you need to be concerned with are your and your kids' physical and emotional health. Energy-draining activities such as trying to maintain a spotless house or whipping up great dinners can wait—a long time.

"I started to think of myself as an orchestra leader and my kids as the musicians in an off-key band," says one mother who's been divorced for three years. "All I ask is that they pick up their instruments and attempt to play along most of the time. I've given up—for my sake and theirs—trying to keep the house as uncluttered as I once did or serving the meals I used to serve when my husband was here. The kids prefer macaroni and cheese anyway." This mother also acknowledges that she probably spends more time, not less, with her kids doing fun things now than she did when married. "If I've got to go out for a quart of milk, I'll take the kids along and maybe we'll stop for pizza. They're too young to stay by themselves, and I can't leave them with their father or have him go out to pick something up now."

The addition of so many roles in your household can be emotionally and physically exhausting if you don't make it a point to maintain other aspects of your personality. Throughout the transition time and later, it's easy to fall into the trap of building your identity around your single-parenthood status, but that can ultimately make you feel isolated and out of the mainstream, rather than a vital part of your community. Spending time with other parents—both married and single—helps solidify and strengthen your sense of yourself as a competent parent, rather than just a struggling single parent. "When my son was born," says one single mother by choice from New York City, "my whole world was being a single mom. I loved every second of it. Now that he's eight, busy in school, in Little League, and the million other things he's up to, I think of myself simply as Jonathan's mom. Our everyday lives make us a regular family. I've got far more in common with other parents than I do with other singles. In fact, being a single mom has become incidental. I'm aware of it only when Jonathan talks about not having his dad living with him. The fact that he knows I'm always willing to talk about whatever's on his mind makes me realize that I've helped create a good family situation for him and for me."

Single parents also need to maintain their work-life identities and adult friendships to retain a healthy self-esteem. "As much as I love being Kate's mom," admits another New York single mother, "I love my work and the excitement and satisfaction it brings me. I really can't imagine not spending the greater portion of my time among other adults who share my interests. Kate's also enthusiastic about what I do. I think her knowing that my life has other dimensions frees her to pursue her own interests without worrying about me."

Over time, you'll find that living in a single-parent home can take on a delightful informality, so that your home becomes a place where people feel comfortable dropping by. You'll notice that you can say yes to invitations without having to wonder if that time, place, and activity is convenient or interesting to another adult. For those who were married, aspects of your personality that you'd subsumed into your former spouse's personality may begin to reemerge. No longer playing "the funny one" to his or her "serious one," you may find a serious side of yourself to like and to be liked. If you are a single parent by choice, you'll notice a big change in yourself and in the reaction of your friends and family to your new status, too. Most who have chosen parenthood knowing at the onset that there would not be a spouse to help out, find that those closest to you rally round once your child has arrived—even if they first were aghast at your plans for nonmarried parenthood. "My boss's first reaction to my announcement that I was pregnant was to suggest that I consider having an abortion. My seventy-five-year-old, very religious aunt, began to cry and said something about my sainted mother turning in her grave. Friends, for the most part, simply thought I'd lost my mind," remembers one Michigan mother. After her daughter was born, she continues, "It was as if everyone was competing to be the most kind, most generous, most loving member of my extended family. And it was sincere." The welcome that her child received has not abated or lessened in any way, she says, adding that not only did those who rejected her idea of single parenthood do a reverse step, but that now most of them wholeheartedly share her belief that she was right to choose to become a mother.

The Uses and Misuses of Wishful Thinking

No matter how well adjusted you and your children are to living in your triangular or straight-line family, it's common for each family member to spend at least some time imagining a square-shaped household. The fantasy of the perfect nuclear family exists all around us, and it's hardly surprising that children are lured by the seeming charm of traditional two-parent family life. Most single parents are well aware that the children fantasize your reunion with your ex-spouse, the return of a deceased parent, or the sudden appearance of a parent they've never known. "We were on the bus one day, on the way to the zoo," notes one never-married mom, "when my four-year-old daughter suddenly blurted out, 'My dad is looking for me, you know. Maybe he'll find me today, because he knows that the zoo is a good place to look.' It gave me the willies. I realized that I had to step up my warnings about not going off with strangers. I was also reminded," says her mother, "of why I have to keep talking about my decision to have her alone, even to the point of letting her know that someday I will help her find her father if she wants to. I guess I can't stop her from wondering now if every man she sees might be him."

Whether or not kids have any kind of relationship with their other parent, they can—and do—create a sort of running tape in their imaginations about the "perfect" mom-and-pop family. Since they live in a mom-*or*-pop household, there are no reminders that two-parent families have their ups and downs, too. In their heads, every down is a direct result of living in a one-parent home. "If my dad were here, he wouldn't make me feed the cat!" is an example of the kind of magical thinking that can fill their heads. But think: Does the same fantasy crop up with surprising frequency for you? Do you also have a running tape, one that activates particularly at times of stress? "If I just had a . . ." and your imagination fills in the blank with this perfect spouse who steps in to save you from the reality at hand. It's this kind of thinking that sells lottery tickets.

Everyone needs a fantasy life of sorts. But there is danger in allowing fantasizing to run amok. No amount of wishing that you were not in this particular family structure will make it so. Fantasies get in the way of living when they take you back to an imagined perfect time in the past, when you fixate on the very best of what was and ignore the normal highs and lows that were reality. Memories that realistically incorporate the past, however, can be useful to strengthen you in the present. Fantasy that you use to visualize where you want to be—what your goals are—can be very therapeutic, and can help you live more fully in the present. Sometimes, fantasy can be useful in and of itself, just for fun.

"One day when my seven-year-old son was in the park with me," says one single mother who lives with her children in a suburb of St. Louis, "he burst into tears." The boy had little contact with his father, who had moved across the country soon after their divorce. "He was crying that he wanted his father. I'd never seen him really miss his dad. Robert seemed always to be such a contented kid. I couldn't conjure up my ex-husband, so I asked Rob what he would be doing right now if his father was with us, and he said they'd be bicycling like all the other kids and their fathers. Well, Rob's father had never been on a bike, as far as I knew, but in Rob's mind that's what fathers and sons did—they rode bikes together. I asked him if he wanted to go to the park with me and ride our bikes. I told him we could pretend that his father was with us. So that's what we did. That night, he told me that, even though he knew it was make-believe, it was the best day in his whole life. I don't think it was so much that he got lost in the fantasy, but that he was glad I acknowledged how he felt."

For kids who don't know their other parent, who either have never met him or her or who don't remember, fantasies can create a safe haven, a way of augmenting and strengthening their identities. It's important that kids be allowed to verbalize their imaginings (they're going to have fantasies whether or not they share them with you). Equally important is that their fantasies originate with them and that your reaction be limited to "that sounds like quite a dad (or mom)," or "I bet it's fun to think about your other parent." You can also share some positive, self-affirming information—"You have brown eyes and strong hands, just like your father"—which can give kids the connectedness they seek.

On the other hand, making up a story that you think will satisfy their need to know something about their other parent—a story that you will have to remember, revise, and ultimately rewrite—is *not* a good idea. Kids do have the right to the truth. Sometimes it's necessary to withhold some of the details. Even parents in two-parent homes don't tell their kids *everything* about each other. But telling outright lies only serves to invite distrust, especially when the lies are about someone with so much imagined or potential impact on their lives. Answering your children's questions honestly and appropriately for their ages is essential. (There is more about this in Chapter 3.)

ESTABLISHING SUPPORT NETWORKS

The African proverb, "It takes a whole village to raise a child," is especially meaningful for single parents. Few solo parents—or their kids—could survive without some help from other caring adults.

Think back to the diagrams of the triangular and straight-line relationships inherent in single-parent families. The intensity created by all of the children's feelings focusing on one parent also results in the kids being especially sensitive to their custodial parent's emotions. To dilute that intensity somewhat, and to provide your children with another outlet for meeting their needs (as well as an outlet for your emotional support needs), you'll do well to expand your family's boundaries to include other caring adults. This is not to suggest that you rush out and remarry. Rather, your goal should be to bring appropriate adult relationships into your children's lives on an ongoing, regular basis—people whom they can know well and care about and who care about them. Although these people exist outside your family's immediate orbit and do not reconfigure the shape of your family into a two-parent square, they do serve to expand your and your children's emotional network.

Your Extended Family

The first people you're most likely to look toward to expand your family boundaries are members of your own extended family. Parents and siblings, in most cases, really are willing to step in and take up the slack for you when you're having a hard time. It's important to nurture these relationships through good times, too, offering an exchange of baby-sitting with your brother's family for a day off for you, or, better yet, getting together as a family to give you and your kids a family-centered get-together.

Don't forget helping your former in-laws maintain contact with their grandchildren, nieces, and nephews, too, if that's at all possible. The importance of maintaining, even strengthening, family bonds is not just to provide you with a reliable backup, but to reassure your children that not all of their connections have been short-circuited and that they are integral parts of a greater whole. Phyllis Diamond, a New York–based family therapist, reminds single parents that the "other" family remains meaningful to your children. "Don't cut them off," she cautions. "This would only compound their losses."

Building a Sense of Community

While blood *is* thicker than water, as they say, it alone does not a family make. You and your children all need loving friends in your lives, and friends can offer a less tangled, but no less strong, safety net. "I really believe that my daughter and I have it pretty good in terms of feeling connected with friends," reports a single mother from San Francisco who runs a publishing business from her home. "Since I work at home, I'm almost always available to pick up another child or two from school when I pick up Lillith, my five year old. It's a lot easier on both of us when I have to keep working and she has a playmate. More often than not, when the mother of the child I'm watching comes to pick him or her up, we wind up chatting for a while, often sending out for Chinese food or pizza and having dinner together. It's always unstructured but gives both Lillith and me a chance to connect to someone else."

Outside your immediate circle of support, you already share a connection with two large communities: other parents and other singles. Community in the form of churches and synagogues, clubs that share your and your children's interests, and support groups all offer connectedness, support, and cohesion. You've got co-workers, neighbors, your children's teachers, coaches, physicians, and friends' parents, and many other passing acquaintances in your realm, even if up until now you've made no strong connections.

The best support—emotional, physical, practical, financial, and otherwise—is mutual support. Make yourself a giving part of each community in which you participate. You may be short on money and have to limit your outings with your kids and other adults, but money is not a prerequisite to helping out at your children's school or other organization that needs volunteers. Volunteering can also help you achieve opportunities for your children that you might otherwise have trouble affording. If you can't afford the dues or cost of uniforms for the scouts, for instance, quietly ask the director if it's possible to barter; you'll type the newsletter, organize the annual picnic, and so forth, in exchange for membership.

If you can't connect with an ongoing group, start one yourself. Therapist Diamond, once a single mother, founded a group that she called Kindred Spirits, for families like her own. Members met for outings with the kids—ice skating in the park, picnics, trips to museums—as well as occasional adults-only activities. "It gave me social plans and it gave the kids a network of friends in similar situations," she notes. "As a single parent, you need someone to nurture you. This is something we can do for each other."

While time is at a premium, the time you take to become part of an activity, particularly one that you can share with your kids and that benefits them, is the best investment you can make. One single father in Wilmington, Delaware, became his ten-year-old son's soccer-team coach, which was difficult for him to fit into his demanding work schedule. "It put a lot of pressure on me to get to practice, but my son was so thrilled to have *his* dad in the limelight. His friends call me 'coach,' which delights him." And a single mom from Arkansas, though short on cash, makes the most of being long on friendships. "Once a month or so, I host a picnic or a potluck and invite everybody. I just tell everyone to bring something, which makes for some interesting combinations of food. But everyone gets fed and we laugh a lot," she says. "Most of all, it gives me and my kids a sense of belonging to a big group of great people."

At times, particularly when you're feeling stressed, it can be tempting to cocoon yourself against the world. While it's not a great idea for any family to be so insulated, it's particularly dangerous for a single-parent family to isolate itself. Your kids need to know that there are others who care about them, who know them well, and to whom they can turn. You need to know this, too.

THE IMPORTANCE OF CREATING STRUCTURE AT HOME

One of the finest gifts that a parent can bring to children is a safe harbor. The world is often unpredictable, meting out rewards one day and disappointments the next. But through good times and bad, the constant in children's lives is the love and support the parent gives them and the safety—emotionally and physically— that they have in their own homes.

One of the most important ways parents can assure their children's own feelings of having a safe harbor is through structure in the home. There is tremendous security for children in knowing what to expect each day and in knowing that their needs and well-being are priorities that are being addressed through household routines.

It's a fact of life in a lot of single-parent homes that there isn't much in the way of daily routine. The lack of structure isn't surprising when you consider the time pressures that single parents experience. The absence of another grown-up reflecting adult standards also leads many single parents to adopt their kids' sense of order—something just short of chaos. On the positive side, a fewer-rule household can give breath to a feeling of free-spirited adventure, as you and your kids learn to snub your collective noses at two-parent-home conventionality. Ironically, however, the randomness can soon become a routine of sorts in itself, one with fewer benefits, requiring more, not less, expenditure of energy. When the lack of structure allows you and your kids to lose track of each other, it carries with it risks to your children's sense of security. As one eighteen year old raised by his mom summed it up: "I didn't really miss having a regular family; what bothered me was that everything was always so up in the air. Some nights we'd have dinner together, but most of the time we'd be grabbing pizzas somewhere. I just wanted some more predictability instead of having to guess every day what was going to happen."

When you are working hard just to keep the family machine running, you can be lulled into believing that your kids—who are seemingly undisturbed by a lack of routine—don't need the safety of a schedule and the pleasure of predictability in their lives. But knowing what to expect is a huge source of comfort for kids, especially those who have experienced an upheaval in their lives.

Setting Up and Maintaining Routines

Routines are, to some degree, a subjective matter, and you'll no doubt want to think through which ones you want as part of your family's living pattern. Make them as easy as possible on all of you. The only important thing is, each day, to have certain touchstones.

Kids are not the only ones to benefit from routine. However exhausted you might get, having the nitty-gritty parts of your day predetermined by an established routine allows you to go on automatic pilot when necessary. You won't waste needed energy or squander valuable time wondering what to do about dinner or when to fit in doing the laundry if you've established regular time slots for needed activities. You simply get it done. One mother of two explains that she considers her family's evening-to-nighttime routine as an integral part of her workday, with each daily event as important as a business meeting. "I don't look at my day as winding down until we've eaten, the kitchen is cleaned up, and the kids are bathed," she says.

A modification of the old adage, "a place for everything and everything in its place," works well for structuring your household. For both your sake and your kids', "a time for everything and everything at its time" should be the order of the day. No particular schedule is better than another; you just need to find the one that's right for you.

There is one routine in particular that you should not compromise, and that is the family dinner. Single parents often express reluctance to eat regularly with their kids, citing frustration at the lack of adult conversation as the reason. But dinner, at the table and together, is central to a family's sense of one another as individuals and as a unit. Sharing a meal, with the attention focused on one another, gives everyone—even if there are just two of you—a chance to interact and each person a chance to talk about what's important to him or her. If you work the evening or night shift, get together daily at breakfast.

There are long-term benefits, as well, to having a regular family mealtime. Researchers at several universities, including George Washington University and Syracuse University, have made some highly insightful discoveries about the homely family dinner. Dr. Steven J. Wolin from George Washington reports in a *New York Times* article that, "if you grow up in a family with strong rituals, you're more likely to be resilient as an adult." He continues that the dinner ritual (as well as other more occasional celebrations, such as holidays) is especially important in homes in which there has been a disruption. Buttressing the case for the ritual of a family dinner is Mary Beth Danielson, co-author of *Reinventing Home*. Quoted in *Child* magazine, she reports that *the* common denominator among National Merit Scholars is that these outstanding teenagers grew up in homes in which families regularly ate dinner together. While raising a scholar may not be high on your list of priorities, this research finding, nevertheless, reveals that a level of confidence and competence is an essential by-product of an established family time.

Certainly, the menu for your family's meal need not be elaborate. To keep kids at the table and to keep you from jumping up to replace the main course with a peanut-butter-and-jelly sandwich for a picky eater, however, each family meal should include something your kids like and will eat. Save trying new foods for side dishes and for company. Also keep dinnertime as pleasant as possible, focusing conversation on family members' interests and activities of the day, not on discipline or criticism. Turn off the TV, since that defeats the purpose of time shared. Vary the format every so often. If your meals tend to be relatively formal, you might want to try having pizza one night a week. If yours are more low-key affairs served on paper plates, try reversing that one night with a dinner on your best plates and with a fancier menu. A regular pattern of sameness with a twist creates ritual upon ritual, something children find entertaining as well as helpful for them to build a sense of the specialness of "our" family.

As to the hour at which you and your family sit down, it's good to be consistent and to remember that earlier is better for most kids. If they're too hungry by the time food is served, they'll be grouches. A too-late dinner also demands that kids wait too long for your attention, and it foreshortens the evening, leaving little time for other necessary and pleasurable routines, including the important task of getting kids to bed on time. "By the time we finished dinner at about eight-thirty," says a New York mom, "we were racing through homework and bath time. Carrie never got to bed before ten and could never wake up in time for school." She notes that by rescheduling dinner to no later than seven, she and her daughter both felt more relaxed.

The Place of "Quality Time" in Routine

Overused to the point of triteness, the term *quality time* was much misunderstood by some two-career parents in the last decade, when they reduced it to interacting with their children by appointment. Obviously these busy parents missed the point, but their confusion doesn't mean you should dismiss the concept of quality time. All parents know that certain times spent with the kids have greater quality than others. The question is how to maximize the quality part.

On the surface, it would appear that the opportunity for quality time with the kids is especially limited for two groups of people: working parents and single parents, both of whom have long daily to-do lists. Since you are single *and* probably working, you may feel you're practically out of the ball park when it comes to finding meaningful hours with your kids. It's true that for many single parents, the pursuit of time with the kids with the simple goal of pleasurable interaction seems daunting. Neil Kalter, author of *Growing Up with Divorce,* observes that the prospect of adding more to a single parent's already crammed calendar, even having fun with the kids, "is so overwhelming many parents end up withdrawing from their children."

The way around that is first to get rid of the term *quality time* forever. Instead, think of it, as William H. Koch, M.D., a child psychiatrist in New York and founder of Skhool for Parents, describes it, as *interactive time.* Then, open your eyes to the opportunities everywhere around you. "Fifteen minutes can do wonders," reports Dr. Kalter. "Look to grab the moments," he advises. Take the kids with you on the errands they enjoy; for little kids this is virtually anything, since the treat is being with you. Older kids generally agree to more entertaining errands such as the car wash and may go along for mundane tasks if they include a pizza stop afterward. Around the house, ask one of your kids to sit with you as you have a quiet cup of tea or come chat while you are sorting laundry. A particularly good conversation starter is having something specific on the agenda, an upcoming birthday party for example, to go over.

Don't overlook the plethora of routine rituals as a source for interactive time. Take a few extra minutes at bedtime to rub a child's back; get up early enough to share breakfast; go for a walk in the evening when the weather is good. Driving anywhere in the car together is frequently a conversation bonus. Sharing a closed space for a defined period of time tends to open up kids for more intimate conversation than you might usually have.

Transition-Time Tips

Certain times of day are rough in any household in which parents work outside the home, which defines the majority of single-parent homes. Specifically, these transition traps are: reconnecting after work, the first day back at work and school after vacation, and any Monday morning.

Meeting your child at the end of the day, whether it's at the child-care center, the after-school program, or at home, creates tension when everyone is least able to handle it. You can reduce the stress by planning ahead. Rather than leaping from your responsibilities at work into your role as parent, try to take a fifteen-minute break, just for yourself, between leaving your job and meeting your children. Stop for a chat with a co-worker, window shop, take a brisk walk. Then you'll be ready in spirit as well as body to reconnect with your kids.

If your daily reunions take place away from home, come prepared with a light snack for your kids if you think they might be hungry. If you need to speak with your child's care provider, wait until after you have greeted your son or daughter with your full attention, letting him or her know that, at this moment, he or she is the most important person in the world to you. Then try not to rush out. Kids prefer moving slowly from one phase of their day to the next. Understand that most kids act up during this transition, for reasons that have little or nothing to do with you. Teachers and child-care workers depend on cooperation from the kids to maintain their effectiveness. While all this good behavior may sit well with your children during the day, once safe with you, they are inclined to vent the restlessness and rebelliousness they may have been storing up all day. A healthy dose of your concentrated attention will help alleviate their symptoms of stress.

Postvacation and Sunday nights have a lot in common, since each embodies the return to attention from at-ease time. The best way to reduce the stress that accompanies these times is to move the schedule back a bit. Return from vacation a full day before you have to return to your regular routine. Start the work- and school-week rhythm early on Sunday evening. Avoid socializing on Sunday nights and keep yourself to the early dinner and bath routines of the work week, helping to ensure that your family greets Monday well rested.

A transition time that is unique to divorced families is that period after the kids have spent time with their other parent. What can you do to make this reunion less emotionally charged? First, remember that your kids take their cues from you. Ask about their activities with their other parent and show enthusiasm for their good times, but don't pry. If your kids prefer to keep details to themselves, respect their wishes. If they seem sullen or out of sorts, let them know you understand that they may be feeling some anger and that you're willing to listen when they want to talk.

When kids return from a visit with a parent they rarely see, the transition can be particularly difficult—for them and for you (not to mention for your ex-spouse pining away for them right now, too). Be patient, and realize that the distress may last for several days or even weeks and can be quite dramatic. Keep in mind that their sadness at missing their other parent isn't a reflection of how they feel toward you. Listen to them, hold them close, and reassure them of both of their parents' love. It can help, too, if you schedule a special outing a few days after their return to sweeten the bitterness somewhat.

GENDER IDENTITY AND ROLE MODELS

Single parents are often called upon to be all things to their children, but there is one responsibility they cannot fulfill, and that is being the opposite-sex parent. Some things simply have to come from a guy. Or a girl. Since there isn't the other-sex parent around to model after, learn from, or learn about, kids in single-parent homes can come up short about ways to form their own separate gender identity. To be sure your children grow up with a strong sense of themselves and the other sex, you must address the issues of gender identity and role models.

The Importance of Role Models

Mothers and fathers are not interchangeable parental figures. Each serves purposes for children that go beyond the love and caretaking inherent in both parent roles. Through the very fact of who they are, male or female, moms and dads display and teach what it is to be that sex. Through their interactions with children, they help kids develop an ability to have comfortable relationships with the opposite sex and with others of their own sex. Additionally, fathers and mothers also tend to bring out and enhance different strengths in children.

Male Role Models

Given that more than eighty-five percent of the single-parent families in this country are headed by women, clearly the role model most in demand is male. Fathers, or meaningful father figures, Dr. Koch points out, help children successfully separate from their mothers, a necessary step to becoming an autonomous adult. Fathers are often more at ease encouraging kids to experiment and to flex their muscles in challenge, especially physical ones. On the playground, many mothers have to rein in a certain anxiety about accidents in order to urge their young children on. Fathers, though, are generally comfortable calling out, "Go to the top, you can do it." One mother in Salt Lake City recalls a small but significant moment that pointed out the benefits of a father figure in helping her child meet a challenge. "My ten-year-old daughter and I were visiting my sister in Phoenix. We were sitting around her pool one afternoon when her husband came out. He's a big, burly man, lots of fun, and very physical. Suddenly he swooped up my daughter and called out, 'I've been wanting to do this all week!' With that, he playfully tossed her into the water. My girl is a good swimmer, but my first impulse was to yell to him to stop, that it would frighten her. I didn't, because I realized this was exactly the kind of thing she needs from her uncles and other men in her life. The sort of jolly attitude that says to her, 'You can do it.' I could tell she was nervous, but she joined in the laughter when she surfaced and she was clearly proud of herself."

Numerous studies show that boys raised without a strong male presence in their lives show insecurity about their gender identity, low self-esteem, and, later in their lives, trouble forming intimate relationships. The problems girls may develop from living without male role models don't usually show up until adolescence or later, and include having difficulty forming successful male/female relationships in adulthood. Victoria Secunda points out in her book *Women and Their Fathers* that learning to love and trust a man requires a leap of faith on these women's part. How much different—or how little—these women's outlooks are from girls raised with at-home fathers, however, isn't really clear. One thing that is apparent, and demonstrated in study after study, is that, as teenagers, girls without fathers or meaningful father figures tend to be more precocious sexually.

Mothers without sufficient or sufficiently good male role models for their children can take some steps on their own to help their girls form healthy male relationships and their sons to understand their own maleness better. It's crucial, say professional observers, that you keep your communication lines open and that you address the issue of sexuality, discussing what is and what is not appropriate. You don't need to preach, but you do need to be sure, through frequent conversations, that your children understand that sexuality is much more than the roles they see played out in the media. Men and women are more multidimensional than the macho or sultry figures they may know from television and movies. Don't shy away from discussing your values openly and often with your sons and daughters, letting them know, for instance, that you want them to behave responsibily toward matters of sexual behavior.

A mother's own attitude about men is another determinant of a daughter's chances of establishing a solid romantic relationship when she grows up and of a son forming a solid opinion of himself. Studies repeatedly show that girls' attitudes toward men, particularly, directly reflect those of their mother. If you are a single mother and you exhibit cynicism and distrust, that's the legacy you are passing on to your children. If you teach them that there are trustworthy, loving, and honorable men—and that such a man is the kind your daughter deserves and your son shall be—their predilection will be to look for or be a man of value.

Nevertheless, there's no question that it's to everyone's benefit to have ongoing, healthy male interaction in your children's lives. If the children's father is not actively involved with them, be sure there are other opportunities for the kids to form relationships with men. Ideally, you have enough extended family in your vicinity to give your children casual and comfortable contact with men who care about them. Friendships with two-parent families also give your kids a chance to familiarize themselves with both men and male/female relationships. Encourage your male friends to spend time around your kids. This advice does not hold true for new boyfriends, however. While they are an obvious source of male companionship for your kids, the wise are wary about how much mixing goes on among kids and boyfriends before the two of you have formed a solid relationship. A great deal of attachment means a great deal of sadness if your relationship doesn't last long. Your kids shouldn't have to go through this again and again. On the other hand, if you are involved in a good partnership, your boyfriend can indeed offer the male modeling your kids need. (For a fuller discussion of your dates and kids, see Chapter 6.)

Female Role Models

Even though a million and a half families are hardly insignificant, the number of children being raised by fathers, put against the number in their mother's custody, makes many single dads objects of awe, curiosity, and sometimes even hostility. "A lot of people act like there is something wrong with the fact that I have custody of Jonathan and Kirsten," complains a single father in Maryland. "Sometimes I think other people feel sorry for my kids, like they are 'stuck' living with their dad instead of their mom."

Most single fathers, like most single mothers, are working hard to bring their children up well, whatever the neighbors may say. These fathers share with their female counterparts many of the same challenges, especially the issues surrounding role modeling. While it is more difficult for single fathers to find each other and have the comfort of comparing notes, it is infinitely easier for them to find female role models for their kids than it is for single moms to find male role models. In addition to the ample numbers of women in child-care centers and schools, sisters, aunts, and cousins, as well as family friends can offer ongoing female companionship to both the daughters and sons of single fathers. Fathers shouldn't be hesitant about seeking these women's presence in their kids' lives. Girlfriends, however, are generally more threatening to kids than they are helpful. Kids typically see them as taking dad away or trying to fill their mother's shoes. But once you have become serious about a woman and your children are more used to her presence, a girlfriend can offer kids valuable insight into the many aspects of being a woman. "My ex-wife was hard-driving, extremely demanding, and critical," recalls a Colorado father of a now-grown daughter. "I was truly relieved when my daughter became close to the woman I was living with for several years. My girlfriend was very mellow and loving. She showed Elizabeth that there was merit in being gentle as well as strong. She had a major influence in the way Liz turned out."

Fathers should be sure they familiarize themselves with some solid principles of parenting. Before, you may have ignored learning about bringing up kids, knowing that your wife was staying up to date with books and magazine articles on the subject. If that was the case, now is the time to enroll in a parenting seminar and pick up a few of those books and "women's magazines" yourself. Make a point of being appropriately involved in your children's school and social activities, even if you find yourself the only dad in attendance. (To help feel less isolated, you might want to join—or perhaps start—a single-dads' support group.) Some fathers must also be careful not to turn well-meaning neighbors and friends into surrogate mothers. Getting women to pitch in with the kids, whether it's for last-minute baby-sitting or inviting your kids along for holiday-cookie bake-offs, is a gift to you and your children. Be sure you don't take it for granted and that you return the favor. Being careful that you do your fair share of helping out with others' children also reinforces for your kids that you are, indeed, a competent parent.

Mothers Raising Sons

For mothers to help sons develop a strong sense of themselves as boys, it is absolutely vital that they arrange for their sons to get plenty of male interaction. Boys are extremely concerned about what a man is and how they fit into the world as a male. Boys of single mothers without male modeling in their lives can develop such insecurity that it's not uncommon for them to drop out of peer relationships in their preadolescent and teen years. Dr. Kalter explains that the boys who lack solid self-confidence about their male identity may become "developmentally stuck" and prefer to hang around the house or with younger kids, instead of pursuing friendships with boys their own age.

As stereotypical as the pursuit may be, you owe it to your sons to expose them to bastions of maleness where the testosterone levels soar. They may or may not choose to follow through with any or all of the male-oriented activities you bring to them, but boys deserve the opportunities these activities offer them to feel good being "one of the guys." Sign your sons up for sports, team and individual, all the ones they are willing to play. (For that matter, involve your daughters in sports, as well, for lots of healthy reasons, including a chance to interact meaningfully with boys and men.) Put them in Cub Scouts, and work alongside to help them earn those badges for tying knots and building campfires.

Be on the lookout for male role models in less obvious places, too. Encourage your sons' friendships with boys who have men in the family—brothers as well as a father—and allow your boys to spend lots of time with them. Whenever you have the choice, opt for a male teacher. Look into Big Brothers, but take care that it is a reputable organization, one that makes careful checks into volunteers' backgrounds. Religious organizations frequently have youth groups for both boys and girls, with any number of parties and outings. Don't overlook the YMCA as well. It can give your boys classes such as karate, in which they'll meet many other boys of varying ages; plus, the Y has relatively low-cost summer-camp programs, including those for boys (or girls) only.

You must also take care not to rob your son of naturally "boyish" behavior. True, there are those who believe boys and girls are born the same, but many parents of sons are hard pressed to say that's so. Boys behave very differently in many ways, and you'll need to watch that you don't view some of these characteristics—their rambunctiousness, for example—as a negative trait. Don't ask your son to play more quietly, "like your sister." Instead, provide him with a superhero cape or the sports equipment he needs, and send him out the door to play. Better yet, join him if he needs someone to pitch or toss. (Be forewarned, though, that throwing "like a girl" may get you tossed out of the game.) Mothers who remember football only as a game to attend on Saturday afternoons in college may have to force themselves to become knowledgeable. It really does help a son feel more camaraderie with you and more comfortable with himself if you learn about activities that interest him. Watch the games together; it's lonely being the only one who is in front of the World Series or who knows what a linebacker is. One mother in New York City ended up accompanying her son to the wrestling matches at Madison Square Garden. "After a while I found myself rooting for one wrestler over another," she says with amazement. If your son's preference is a quieter game such as chess, learn that too. Let him take the lead in his favorite activities, explaining aspects of them to you, for a change (which you may well need anyway). And if it's his nature to be quiet and/or gentle, let him know that you value these qualities, too.

Especially as your son grows older, be careful not to relegate "men's jobs" to him on a regular basis. It doesn't benefit any of you for Mom to become inept in the face of problems usually tended to by Dad. Being the "man of the house" is also too great a burden for any child to have to carry.

When your girlfriends are around, make sure all of you avoid male-bashing. One Florida mother, whose son was just five when she and her husband broke up, recalls an afternoon when she and some of her women friends were complaining about their current men. "One of the women was really disparaging men, but in a very funny way," she says. "We were all getting a big laugh out of it until I looked over at my son, who was then seven. He was absolutely crestfallen. When I thought about the message we were sending him about his own kind, I felt pretty bad, too."

When your sons start edging toward adolescence, look for—and find—ways to talk to them about how their bodies will soon be changing. The maturation of young girls may be more outwardly dramatic, but for boys, the onset of erections and nocturnal emissions (around the age of twelve or so) is a source of curiosity and sometimes profound embarrassment. Be matter-of-fact about how and when their bodies will probably change, but be empathetic as well. Find a context, such as your brother's experiences and reactions or perhaps something relevant you saw in a movie, to ease your boys' discomfort and reassure them that the changes and their responses to them are normal. You should also bear in mind that, as sons mature, there is a real temptation to become more flirtatious with them. Laughter and joy in each others' presence is always welcome; flirting, however, pushes past acceptable parent/child boundaries.

Fathers Raising Daughters

In the earlier years, the job of single dads raising daughters is eased somewhat by the numerous women in all children's lives, the child-care providers and schoolteachers, as well as the women in their extended families. That's all to the good, of course, but it doesn't get fathers entirely off the hook. Like moms raising sons, you too may have to go out of your way to discover with your daughter the pleasures of girlish play. Should your preschool daughter have strong preferences about the way she dresses (all kids this age, including boys, tend to display this characteristic) respect them. If she wants only frilly dresses and French braids for a time, let her have them. Don't worry, conversely, if she wants to wear only jeans and have her hair pulled back with barrettes. The point is to allow her to be comfortable with the way she is.

However, as you work to allow your daughter her femaleness, don't fall into the trap of assigning her certain chores because society has viewed them as "women's work." Don't try to turn your daughter into your housekeeper. As your young girl nears preadolescence, you have other important responsiblities facing you. Seek out reliable and complete information about how and when females mature physically, and be prepared to deal with your own daughter's maturation sooner than you might assume. Only a few decades ago, menarche, the onset of periods, generally occurred in girls at age thirteen; now it more often appears at age eleven or twelve and sometimes in girls even younger. You should have all the information you need to answer your girl's questions, and if telling your daughter about how adolescence will affect her body totally unnerves you, let her ask a woman with whom she is close address the issue with her. But make it clear to your daughter that even if it does make you somewhat uncomfortable, you are happy to discuss female sexuality with her at any time. You may need the same kind of help when it comes time to buy your daughter her first bra. Most young girls find that a grueling experience with their mothers. Buying a bra with their dad might put them over the edge.

Be aware, too, of how you may react to your daughter's new physical maturity. Many fathers, including those who were close to their daughters before adolescence, become confused and uncomfortable about how to treat their daughters as newly sexual creatures. As a result of their dilemma, some fathers withdraw emotionally and physically from their girls. The result is a daughter who is suddenly and abruptly cut off from her dad and without any idea why. It is extremely painful for a girl to experience a father's rejection—which it is in her eyes—and she will probably blame herself. This most often comes at a time when girls are starting to be interested in boys. You can imagine the dramatic effect that isolating yourself from your daughter would have on her self-confidence. A girl who feels loved and accepted by her dad doesn't need to pursue love and acceptance from every boy she meets.

Of course, your daughter's development changes some of your physical relationship. With her emerging sexual maturity, fondling, kissing, tickling, and lap-sitting appropriately diminish (if indeed those actions hadn't waned long before). Hugs are always great, as are father/daughter kisses. But if you find yourself physically stimulated by any interaction, however innocent, it's time to rethink the boundaries. Again, don't just close yourself off. Be upfront with your daughter: She is becoming a woman and this may call for a change in the way you treat one another physically. Use a conversation of this nature to increase the emotional closeness you share. Be sure your girl understands that any altering of your behavior toward her is in keeping with her maturation and not a form of punishment or withdrawal on your part. Reassure her that the love and emotional closeness between you remains solidly intact.

Sharing a Bed and Household Privacy

Many single parents find it comforting to sleep with their kids, at least now and then. This is unquestionably an issue that opposite-sex parents must consider, but the rules concerning sleeping in the same bed really apply to children of both sexes. Most experts agree that kids beyond the preschool years need the independence and strength that comes from knowing they can sleep by themselves, apart from the parent. However, this is particularly true for preadolescent boys being raised by their moms. Dr. Kalter points out in his book that boys who sleep in the same bed with their mothers tend to be more confrontational with them during the day. Dr. Kalter suggests that daytime skirmishes may result from the boy's need to make a dramatic show of being separate, since he finds the nighttime closeness so satisfying. It may also reflect his guilt about the sexual pleasure he enjoys from sleeping next to his mother. The sexual undertones for both sons and daughters are yet another reason why experts frown on the family's sharing a bed.

You, too, may find that sharing a bed with your kids nurtures in you an inappropriate dependence on your children for warmth and comfort. When the kids ask to climb into your bed, try another approach. Sit on their bed with them for a time to give them an extra dose of togetherness. Then go off to your own bed. Alone.

Parents raising opposite-sex children eventually must deal with the issues around household privacy as well. While you want children to be comfortable with their bodies and with the idea of the opposite-sex body, it can be quite uncomfortable at times, such as when your child bursts in during your bath. Respect for each other and your personal privacy is part of what you'll need to address here. Teaching your children to honor your privacy is teaching good manners and also establishing that you are all indeed separate people who deserve respect. Again, the other issue involved here is that of sexual stimulation for your children. Even preschoolers (and children virtually from birth, many experts say) are sexual creatures who are subject to sexual excitement. They don't recognize it as such, but too much sexual stimulation is unhealthy for them.

You don't need to hide from your opposite-sex children, but don't make it common for them to have access to your nudity. Should they encounter you emerging from the shower, for example, tell them quietly that this is private time for you and to please leave. Obviously, parading naked around the house or in your underwear is not a good idea. Don't make a big deal of this—you don't want to create shame around sex or nudity—but do remember that kids tend to be prudes when it comes to their parents' behavior. It's healthier for them for you to tilt toward conservatism. Likewise, respect your children's need for privacy, practicing the same behaviors—knocking before entering their rooms and staying out when they're using the bathroom, for example—that you expect from them.

PROFESSIONAL POINT OF VIEW

LYNN LEIGHT, Ph.D., author of *Raising Sexually Healthy Children*, is founder and executive director of seventeen Sex, Health, Education (S.H.E.) Centers nationwide. She appears often on television and as a guest lecturer, addressing the issues of children and sexuality.

Q. We all want our children to have a healthy sense of sexuality, but how, exactly, would you define that?
A. A healthy sense of sexuality means having a clear sense of identification within your gender role, but also being able to see yourself as a total being. Ideally, you can dance comfortably in either of the behavior arenas we classify as male or female. You can be aggressive and mellow, soft and hard. Boys generally strug-

gle with the issue of gender identification more than girls. Boys spend most of their lives trying to understand what it is to be a man. Even in two-parent families, if the father is distant or away a lot, the child will still struggle with his identity.

Q. How do children learn about the sex of the parent they don't live with, especially if they don't see much of that parent?
A. In their effort to understand maleness, boys are constantly seeking out role models. They look for those men who have gained the respect of others, which is why they love superheroes so much. A mother raising a son alone must help him in his search for appropriate role models, especially as her son approaches adolescence. If there are no men to be close to in the extended family, the mother must grab whatever bits and pieces of male modeling for her son that she can. She shouldn't be indiscriminate about it—in desperation, some women turn their sons over to just about anyone, appropriate or otherwise. Various organizations, religious groups, or ones for single parents, like Parents Without Partners, can offer responsible male companionship. Literature is full of wonderful role models, and watching certain television shows or movies together presents more opportunities to examine role models. Mom should follow up with a dialogue with her son concerning these men's behaviors and reactions; she can help lead him to developing a good sense of how men should act.

Dads raising daughters on their own have a tough time, especially in this paranoid world that misinterprets even an embrace. Girls need same-sex role models just as much as boys do, but women who can be a part of a girl's life are generally in greater supply than are men. If necessary, fathers should lean on family members to be and stay involved with their daughters.

Q. Is it better for kids to get their information about sex from the same-sex parent? Are there ways to help them be more comfortable during these potentially embarrassing conversations?
A. There has been an enduring myth that dads had to tell sons, and mothers their daughters about sex. It's perfectly fine for the other-sex parent to be the one telling. Even though mothers and

fathers have never walked in the other sex's shoes, they can help a child understand his or her feelings by saying, "This is what I heard about how it feels from the men/women I know." If parents feel awkward in these discussions, they should be candid about it. Inject some humor into the conversations and tell the kids they are giving them information they wished they had had at their age. Parents should also look for books as resources, so that children can more easily frame questions about what they don't understand.

Q. If children don't ask a parent much about sex and sexual development, should a parent boldly bring up the subject?
A. Absolutely! Don't wait for others to become your children's educators. They won't give the information you want them to have. Use any opening you come across to convey information about sex. If you pay close attention, you'll find that there are many times when your kids ask a casual, seemingly unrelated question, or you see something on TV that opens the way for you to give your kids valuable information about sex and their bodies. I refer to those moments as "golden opportunities," and I urge parents to watch for and take advantage of them as they come your way. Don't worry that you might be telling your kids too much at any one time. Kids absorb only what they can handle. And be very clear that your door is always open for any question they might have, and that the dialogue between you about sex and sexuality is an ongoing one.

Q. Is the lack of a loving male/female relationship in a home something that creates long-lasting problems for the children who grow up with a single parent?
A. No. Love is love is love. A loving parent is constantly demonstrating what love is all about in many gestures and kindnesses every day. Growing up with a loving single parent is certainly healthier for children than being in a home in which love is insincere and parents smile through gritted teeth. One area single parents who are divorced must watch, though, the one thing that could damage children, is denigrating the other parent. That really hurts kids.

Q. What can a single parent do to teach children about healthy male/female relationships, especially if he or she is not involved in any ongoing ones while the kids are growing up?

A. Kids should see that you are a whole person, whether you are in or out of a relationship, and that you are filling your life with nourishing activities and with people you like and who share common interests with you. So many children see parents who long for a relationship and sacrifice themselves just to have one. The best way to find the right life partner, and what children should see, is doing the best for yourself.

Parents can help kids learn more about the dynamics of couple relationships by observing the ones in their spheres—the neighbors, relatives, friends—with their kids. Develop ongoing discussions about what all of you like and don't like in the way these couples function together. Relate to incidents from a male and female perspective and then bring it back to home base by asking the children if they have been in similar situations and how they would like to have had the situation handled. Relationships are everywhere around us and we can learn from all of them.

3

Family Management

Probably the biggest asset a single parent can have is the determination to make the family situation work. This "can-do" attitude framed by a positive outlook may sound hokey, but it is a mistake to underestimate the power it brings you. It both energizes and focuses you. Even on the worst days, it helps you get out of bed in the morning, and that's something to be grateful for right there.

The way you act on determination is by taking charge. As the sole adult on the premises, you occupy the executive office anyway, so you may as well get comfortable with the role. There will be times when you feel the kids are the ones inside the Oval Office with their feet on the desk, but it doesn't have to be that way. The first order of business is creating the communication network which will assure that all family members are being heard—and are hearing. Next, you need to have your discipline philosophy and techniques firmly in place and clear to you and the kids. Finally, there is your family as a team, each doing his or her bit to keep this family moving smoothly along.

COMMUNICATING WITH YOUR KIDS

Something quite wonderful happens in families in which conversation has an honored place. Though single parents may yearn for the more sophisticated banter that other adults provide, there's a lot of mutual pleasure to be found in parent-child exchanges. Much of your conversation with the kids, of course, is in the form of directives: "Clean your room," "Show me your homework," "Find your sneakers." Necessary but not illuminating to anyone. But your single-parent status provides you with an extra opportunity to share your thoughts and for you to impart your values in words, simply because you and they are more likely to turn to each other for talk, both small and otherwise. And there's a bonus: Because there is more interactive dialogue in the single-parent home, children in such homes, in general, absorb a higher level of speaking and listening skills and are more verbal than children living in a two-parent family.

Helping Kids Communicate

Creating an environment that allows for free-flowing, natural conversations with your children really begins before children can talk. But it's never too late to develop the art. To do it well, you've got to be quiet more often than you might want. This can be hard for you as a single parent, because you may be so emotionally bound to your kids that you may think you have the right and the obligation to know everything that's on your children's minds, or that they need to know all that's on your mind.

To be sure, children prattle a lot, and no reasonable parent would or could listen all day with full attention. Learning to tune kids out when necessary, however, can lead to ignoring what they have to say more often than you should. When your child is elaborating on the inner workings of some video game, go ahead and concentrate on something that matters more to you, keeping just enough attention focused to catch any important information. But when a child is giving you information or just hints about his day, his thoughts, his friends, his feelings, or anything else of substance, be prepared to really listen. You don't have to stop what you're doing and steady yourself for an "important" talk. In fact, continuing to cook dinner while a child talks can keep her talking.

If there's something about your children's world that *you* want to talk about, or you think your kids want to discuss but don't know how to begin, try the method suggested by Dr. Kalter, saying, for instance, "Some kids whose parents don't live together worry that . . ." instead of asking directly what your children are thinking. Too-broad questions, such as, "What's on your mind?" are apt to be answered "nothing," nearly one hundred percent of the time. Be careful of slipping into "psycho-speak," however. Kids pick up instantly your attempt at being a pseudo-shrink. Most resent it and are apt to tune out anything that sounds like you're reading a script from the latest child-psychology text.

The subject of the other parent, of course, does need to be addressed on a fairly continual basis, and it is up to you to set the tone. Your children need to know that you are always willing to listen, nonjudgmentally, to their questions and their comments about their other parent. Keep in mind that you and your children may not always share the same view of your family's configuration. When you're feeling positive and even joyful about being a single parent, your children may be down and sad. On the other hand, you may be feeling more anxiety about your single-parent status than do your kids. So keep talking—and listening.

No matter how children came to be living with just one parent, they need to be told, again and again, that your family's configuration is the result of an adult decision or an act of fate that has nothing whatsoever to do with them. Divorced parents must take special care to repeat this truth, and it's best if both parents make the statement clearly and repeatedly. And, as difficult as it might be, keep any bitter remarks to yourself about your ex-mate. If your kids are expressing their own bitterness, it's tempting to join in; however, this is not the time to develop camaraderie. When your children's other parent is not living up to his or her obligations, explain that, "He (or she) loves you as much as he (she) is able to. That may not be as much as either of us want for you, but it's the best he (she) can do."

Do not make a point of how much better a parent you are. Remember: Children will also be anxious about their relationship with their noncustodial parent, and it's up to both you and your ex to help put them at ease. However much you may resent The Other, that person is still your children's parent and will always be. Furthermore, part of that person is part of your children. As hard as it may be, do not regale your children with tales, true or not, of their other parent's shortcomings. Refrain from it for no other reason than that, in the end, it harms your children more than it can ever harm your ex-spouse. As Michael Lewis, Ph.D., director of the Institute for Child Development and Psychiatry at the Robert Wood Johnson Medical School in New Jersey, points out, children seldom start to hate one parent because of the wrathful words of the other. Instead, they turn the anger inward. "They learn," he says, "to despise those parts of themselves that are like the other parent." You don't have to sing the praises of the spouse who has let you down, but keep the bitter remarks to yourself and to private discussions with your friends.

Single parents who have never married, or whose ex-spouses are long gone from the scene, with little likelihood of reappearing, may feel compelled to make up a story to satisfy a child's need to know about his or her other parent. That would be a mistake, say a number of prominent child psychologists and pediatric psychiatrists in an article published by *Working Mother Magazine*. (The article was a response to a suggestion made by Dr. T. Berry Brazelton at the American Academy of Pediatrics conference in 1982 that single mothers by choice could make up a fantasy figure with whom the child could identify.) While each respondent stressed that the information given should be true, all agreed that the truth need not be complete and should always include the fact that, "He and I left each other; he didn't leave you," or "I decided to have you by myself and your father had nothing to do with my decision." If you have warm feelings about your child's father, you can share them, look at photographs together, and help him or her develop a sense of who the father is or was. Strongly negative feelings should not be shared, but they shouldn't be whitewashed either.

Whatever information you give must be appropriate to your

child's level of understanding. At two years old, for instance, a child can be assured that she has a father who "lives in another town." At four, he might feel better if you allow him to create *his* own fantasy ("If you could make up a dad, what would he be like?" you can ask). Jane Mattes, founder of Single Mothers by Choice, suggests saying, "You're curious about your father," or even, "What a good question!" when a child asks to know more about his or her other parent as a way of letting your child know that you are always willing to listen and to help him sort things out.

To keep the subject of the other parent alive in your home, read books together that depict a variety of family configurations, including some that have moms and dads and kids in them. When watching television, look for opportunities to discuss mom and dad roles. (Some single mothers try to avoid the subject of daddies altogether, but this denies children information about fathers that they need to learn.) Just keep conversations simple and straightforward, always leaving room for more questions to emerge as your children grow and their need for answers grows with them.

One last thing: It's sometimes tempting for single mothers by choice to tell a child that he doesn't need a father. That explanation, which has the temporary effect of making your family appear "normal" and simply one of many possible types of families, can backfire. No son needs to believe that, when he becomes an adult, he, by nature of his sex, is expendable to a family. Daughters, too, can be shortchanged by any hint that men are merely sperm donors in a family.

If your children aren't verbalizing their feelings or aren't responding to your invitations for conversation, there are other approaches that can help them open up. A technique that a number of therapists recommend is to have kids create a picture book or photo album that represents how they feel. There are also numerous books, designed for kids from preschool age through young adult, that deal with issues your kids may want to discuss but need more information in order to organize and express their thoughts. Some are in workbook format and thus encourage kids to express themselves by writing instead of by talking, an easier approach for many kids. Regardless of what method you use to help your kids to open up, just be careful not to push kids into an activity that you choreograph. Provide the interest and the permission to go ahead with the project, but let the activity be theirs.

What Kids Tell Their Friends about Your Family

Helping kids communicate goes beyond getting them to talk to or listen to you. For kids who live with one parent, learning to respond to friends' innocent (and sometimes mean-spirited) questions about their nonresident parent requires some special attention. "My daughter was not quite three when a friend of hers who spends a lot of time in our apartment demanded to know where Callie's dad was," reports a never-married mom. "This playmate didn't know any other kids in single-parent homes. If I'd been prepared for my daughter facing this sort of interrogation, I may have jumped right in, saving Callie from having to come up with any explanation of her own. But before I could say anything, Callie said, 'He doesn't live with us.' And that was that. The two kids went right back to playing." This mom adds that it hasn't always remained as easy for her daughter as it was that first time. "One time, she responded to a kid in the park by pointing to a man a distance away, saying that was him. Another time, when the Gulf War was in the news, I overheard her telling a new friend that her dad was a soldier. We talk a lot about why her father isn't with us, and I answer all her questions honestly. But that doesn't always make it easier for her to talk to her friends, almost all of whom live with two parents. When she decries not having a father at home, I empathize, but I always remind her that I'm glad I'm her parent." This mother concludes that no matter how much she and her daughter have come to a certain comfort level between themselves in discussing her child's father, the issue is constantly being renewed for her daughter in her relationships with her peers.

How your children respond publicly to questions about their other parent reflects not only their own comfort and confidence but their level of maturity. A young child, even one who is feeling good about his or her situation, may respond with fantasy. Don't take this as a sign that he or she is emotionally distraught over the reality of your family life. But it might be a signal that your child needs some help from you in formulating a script with which he is comfortable. Whatever the particulars, it is important to help your child learn to explain as truthfully as possible the circumstances that led to his or her living with you as sole on-site parent. As one single mother puts it, "Helping Jess say that his dad moved out and now has another wife states clearly that Jess has nothing whatsoever to be ashamed of. If I helped him make up a prettier story, it would be like telling him that he had some awful secret. Now, when his dad comes to visit him once a year, Jess doesn't have to worry about anything he's said to his friends colliding with reality."

Making Yourself Heard

"I called it *talking,* but Lillian said I was always nagging," says a mom who shares custody of her eleven-year-old daughter with her ex-husband. "I had to admit that Lillian and I were often locked in battle, while she seemed better able to handle talking with her dad. So I asked him what his secret was. This very man—the one who'd refused to go to marriage counseling—told me he had been attending parenting classes at the Y. I signed up the next week." In her class, she learned a strategy that child-development experts have been expounding for some time. "The results of learning to rephrase my feelings from accusations to 'I-statements' are almost miraculous," Lillian's mother now says. What are I-statements?

I-statements are nonjudgmental appraisals of a situation that allow you to communicate how you feel and why you feel that way. Like many parents who find your kids' clothes scattered throughout the house—again—you may be reduced to screaming, "Why are you kids such pigs? Pick up these clothes now!" Chances are that the kids will retreat, tuning you out, except for the part when you called them pigs. Not only does this give them license to use name-calling when they're angry, it does nothing for

FIVE TIPS TO GET YOUR CHILDREN TO LISTEN

1. WHISPER. Kids learn to tune out yelling pretty early on. But when you lower your voice to barely audible, they have to focus their attention to hear you.

2. WRITE A NOTE. Children don't get a lot of mail, and a letter saying what's on your mind gives kids a chance to hear you out without the opportunity to interrupt.

3. TELL THEM WHAT'S ON YOUR MIND on subjects that have nothing whatsoever to do with big issues. For example, if something strikes you as funny about a video you're watching with your kids, tell them why. It will give them an insight into your particular sense of humor and will encourage them to share their own quirky humor. In other words, let small talk be valued.

4. DON'T DISCUSS IMPORTANT ISSUES DURING THE HEAT OF AN ARGUMENT. If the conversation you and your children are having deteriorates into a shouting match, call a time-out. Say that this is too important to be discussing when you're both so angry, and then set a time for resolving the issue.

5. TALK AT BEDTIME. Kids are thrilled to extend their day for any reason, including listening to you. Of course, don't bring up subjects or use a tone of voice that could upset them and interfere with everyone's getting a good night's sleep.

engendering a positive self-image. Nor is it likely to result in their remembering to pick up their clothes. By rephrasing your need for order by using an I-statement, you greatly increase your chances of being heard. Next time, try saying: "When you don't put your clothes where they belong, I get upset." No one's been accused of anything. No one's been attacked. You've simply stated your case. Similarly, instead of accusing your child of being dumb or thoughtless for leaving her roller skates on the front steps, try saying, "When you leave your skates on the steps, I get worried because someone might fall on them." When you use I-statements, you put the responsibility where it belongs, you address the behavior you want changed without implying (or stating) that there is something wrong with your children themselves.

Other forms of switching gears can work wonders, too. After all, sometimes when we replay the same old record (or is it now a CD?), we stop paying attention to the words. "I had told Jeremy about a thousand times to put his bike away in the garage, not in the driveway," says one mom. "Finally, in a burst of ingenuity, I decided to let the bike speak for itself. I attached a note to the handlebar for Jeremy to find. It read: 'Dear Jeremy, I am afraid of being stolen. I am afraid of rust (ick!) I am afraid that Mom will drive over me. Please, put me in a safe place. Love, your bike.' " This mom reports that by adding a little humor to the situation, she was able to avoid yet another confrontation and, better yet, her note resulted in Jeremy properly locking his bike in the garage.

DISCIPLINING ON YOUR OWN

Probably the most difficult part of being a parent is discipline, and if it's 100-percent true for parents together, it's 110-percent true for single parents. However, as a single parent you do have the opportunity to decide for yourself the rules you care about and how you are comfortable enforcing them. You should also relax about your status as a single parent in relation to your effectiveness as a parent. The Temple University study referred to in Chapter 1 concluded that the parenting by single parents was every bit as effective as that by their married counterparts of equivalent educational and socioeconomic levels.

As you give serious thought to your discipline techniques, be sure you have a working knowledge of normal child development. At some ages, kids can be much more difficult to handle than they are at others. You might worry that you are a failure in the discipline department, when in fact your kids' difficult behavior may be a result of a totally normal developmental phase. Being familiar with the phases and stages kids go through can be especially helpful for you as a single parent. Teachers, friends, and family members may overreact to some of your children's behaviors or moods, blaming what may not be at all amiss on the fact that your kids are from a single-parent home. Your best defense is some sure-footed knowledge about kids' normal behavior. One of the best series of books on child development is from the Gesell Institute of Human Development, co-authored by Louise Bates Ames, Ph.D. These start with *Your One Year Old,* and run through to *Your Ten to Fourteen Year Old.* Each of these titles illustrates typical developmental behavior for boys and girls of a particular age group.

As the sole disciplinarian, your major hurdle is apt to be the lack of down time. No longer can you pass some problems on with the "Wait until your father gets home" cliché. Everything is in the single parent's lap. "When my daughter starts whining because she wants candy before dinner, it doesn't matter how tired I am, how bad my day was, or what important phone calls I have to return immediately," reports a single father of a four year old in Tulsa. "There is almost never even one discipline situation I can put off handling because something might be happening with me," he adds.

Single parents also talk about how difficult it is being the sole family sentry, because it means they play both good guy and bad guy, roles two parents on the premises can pass back and forth. This quandary is more tolerable if you rethink the purpose of discipline. A true understanding of discipline and its real purpose will help you realize that there is no need for the roles of good guy–bad guy, but, instead, for a "strong" guy, with a consistent and clear set of rules.

Contrary to popular thought, discipline is the *management* of children's behavior. It is not punishment, the part of discipline with which it is often confused. "Discipline is an act of love," explains Dr. Koch. "Parents often feel guilty setting and enforcing the rules, but, in the long run, kids see a lack of rules as a lack of love." Echoing Dr. Koch's professional observation is Alexandra, a twenty-nine-year-old Texan. Raised by divorced parents, she is now a single mother of a toddler and tries hard to be consistly firm. "Throughout my growing-up years I kept waiting for someone to say no to me, and no one ever did," she says with a sigh. "I always felt that if they really loved me, they would have taken the time and effort to give me rules. I'm not going to make the same mistake with my child."

Discipline Basics

Although the subject of discipline seems to be endlessly fascinating to parents, the basic structure of effective discipline isn't complex at all. Keeping behavioral order in your home will be easier if you stick to the following few, but ironclad, principles.

Establish and Maintain Clearly Defined Limits. The foundation on which all discipline rests is well-established limits. Having clear limits is something that benefits all children. Like structure, having limits helps children feel secure. They know what is expected of them and what will happen if they overstep the boundaries. Children without limits will push and push, with behavior ever more outrageous, in a struggle to find what the boundaries are. This stresses everyone—parents, children, and anyone with the misfortune to be around them. There are more than unhappy immediate consequences to no limits. A study of permissive parenting conducted by Dr. Diana Baumrind at the University of California at Berkeley shows there are unhappy long-range consequences as well. In the study, children who came from homes that were loving but too permissive lacked confidence and were considered at high risk for later antisocial behavior.

Maintain Your Parental Authority. Some parents find the mantle of authority an uncomfortable one. Single parents in particular may have trouble maintaining themselves as authority figures because of underlying guilt; they feel a continuing sense that they have deprived their kids of the second parent, and so they tend to give in to the children's requests, even when unreasonable.

To some extent an ambivalence about authority may also result from a misunderstanding of a parenting approach made popular in the sixties and seventies. Haim Ginnot, among other child-rearing experts, advocated that parents understand children's problems from the kids' point of view. This humanistic approach to raising kids was rightly well received, but over the years some parents have turned a kinder style of child rearing into an excuse to give up parental authority. As the parent, you *must* be the one in control. Families are not democracies and the voices are not equal among parents and children. The leader's voice is yours. That doesn't give you license to abuse power, but it sharply defines the lines of authority. The kids won't love you any less for being a parent instead of a pal. They probably have plenty of pals; parents are harder to come by.

Keep the Rules Few in Number and Be Willing to Renegotiate as Your Kids Mature. The most effective way to set up the rules is to have only a few of them and make them reasonable for each child's age. Pick out three or four areas in which it is important to you to have the kids' compliance. These might include, among others, the principle of treating you and other adults with respect, the task of doing homework, a reasonable bedtime (something that is particularly difficult in many single-parent homes), and a cap on the hours and types of shows the kids may watch on TV. Once you have a general framework in place, you won't be worn down by constant fights about daily functioning. This frees you to negotiate other issues as they come up. A word of warning for those tempted to put off this task: Research also shows that, unless you have established discipline in your home by the time kids are age nine or so, effective discipline is extraordinarily difficult to achieve. After that age, children are unresponsive to most discipline efforts.

The Art of Negotiation

To raise children successfully requires that you constantly reevaluate your kids' changing abilities and growing autonomy. Arthur Gray, Ph.D., a New York City psychologist who frequently works with young people, points out that this runs throughout the entire child-rearing process. "In a healthy parent-child relationship, the parent is always pushing the limits outward to keep pace with the child's growing maturity," he notes. For example, you might decide to let your toddler walk in front of you on a quiet street instead of holding his hand. You may allow your second-grader to go to the school bus stop alone. Many times kids move forward in what they are allowed to do because it is clear to a parent that they are now capable. As kids get older, however, many start wanting to be an active negotiator in matters concerning what they are and are not allowed to do.

There are three essential types of parenting: authoritarian, authoritative, and permissive. In authoritarian homes, the parent's word isn't questioned. In permissive homes, the parent's word is seldom heard. It's the authoritative home, the family with the type of discipline we are discussing, that serves the children best. Although the parent is definitely the authority figure, the children have some say-so in many situations because negotiation is part of the family's discipline structure.

All parents need negotiating skills with teenagers, but single mothers raising sons are apt to find negotiation an invaluable asset even before their boys become teens. As boys enter pre-adolescence, around age nine, single mothers often find that they have a new personality on their hands. No longer sweet, compliant children, many boys at this age begin to dig in their heels and answer most of their mother's requests with a reverberating No! "My son had always been stubborn, but other than that, he was such an easy child," recalls a single mother in New Jersey. "Almost from the first day of fourth grade, he became impossible. He wouldn't do anything I said; he even refused to go to school if he didn't feel like it. I actually carried him to school one morning."

Dr. Kalter describes an internal conflict with which he reports all boys being raised in a single-mother household wrestle. "On the one hand, they tend to feel that they have to rely on their mother for the parenting support and love they realistically still need. Yet they are notably uneasy about giving in to the usual demands parents make of children, because doing so feels tantamount to being a 'momma's boy,' a 'wimp,' or, worse, 'effeminate.' " The availability of male role models (see Chapter 2) helps resolve this conflict for boys, because they have the opportunity to witness firsthand that it isn't necessary to buck authority to establish their identity. Having other males in their lives also helps them feel more comfortably part of the gender, and that makes them less conflicted. But to get along better with your boys on a day-to-day basis, mothers had better be prepared for some give and take, what Dr. Kalter calls "reasonable compromise."

Negotiation, once you get into it, can be fun in the way some games are fun. Be sure you are crystal clear about your bottom line, which is the boundary you are establishing for your child. How you get to the boundary is where your ingenuity comes in. As an example, ten-year-old Jeffrey was getting headaches from playing his new video games so much over Christmas vacation. When his mom told him he would have to give up the games for a while, it was instantly apparent that a straightforward, laying down the law about the issue would create a battle between the two of them. The bottom line, his mom quickly ascertained, was that Jeffrey had to limit the amount he played. "We have a problem," she started out. "In order for you not to have any more of those headaches, you will have to limit yourself to only two hours of video games for the whole day. How would you like to do it—an hour in the morning and one in the afternoon, or four half-hour sessions throughout the day?" By starting off with "we have a problem," Jeffrey's mother immediately established the two of them as a team. From there on, the underlying dynamics of the negotiation were much less threatening to Jeffrey. He didn't feel like a "weenie," because his mom allowed him to have genuine input in the problem's resolution.

A concrete way of negotiating with all of your children is the drawing up of contracts, especially when you're considering specific behaviors. For example, for your daughter's privelege of riding her bike without you escorting her, write up together the rules that she must follow, such as wearing a helmet, riding only with friends and never alone and the like.

Ways to Contain Your Battles

secret that raising kids is as hard a job as you can find. However rewarding kids may be, they are also frustrating, demanding, and sometimes infuriating. Given the nature of the one-on-oneness of single parent to child (even when there are siblings) in your family, it's not surprising that disagreements sometimes slide directly into face-off confrontations. By keeping the following in mind, you should be able to avoid the fray most of the time.

Don't Set Yourself Up for Unnecessary Fights. While consistently enforcing the rules is probably the most important part of keeping the peace, a measure of flexibility is in order as well. You also have to evaluate each child individually, to be sure the rules are appropriate for the child's personality and temperament. For instance, your knee-jerk refusal to your eight year old's request to stay out playing later may be based on an older sibling's lack of responsibility at the same age. (Admittedly, this is tricky territory, since the charge of "unfair!" is almost a given. The way around that is to be sure you are giving consideration to each child's individual strengths and needs.) If your child's request is reasonable or seems to be, on the surface, at least hear it out.

Look for the Underlying Reason Behind Disagreeable Behavior. Before you take it personally, remember that your child's testiness may have nothing to do with you. The surliness may spring from his anxiety about something scheduled for later in the day, a test, a social event, or it may just be age-appropriate behavior. Assuming the child has a relationship with the other parent, could something be happening there? The single mother of a six year old tells about his unruly behavior one Sunday night, and her insight into it: "As soon as Ned came back from the weekend with his dad, I knew he was in a rotten mood. He fought me on everything, from getting into his jammies, to turning off the TV, to brushing his teeth. I was about ready to blow when I stopped to consider that it was unusual for him to be so relentlessly obstinate. I asked him if he'd like to have a glass of milk at the table with me and talk for a few minutes before he got into bed. He seemed relieved and agreed immediately. It turned out that his dad was terribly depressed that weekend because his girlfriend was breaking up with him. Ned felt overwhelmed with sadness for his dad, but there was nothing he could do to help his father feel better. With all that Ned had going on inside of him, it was no wonder he was such a grouch when he got home."

Look for Underlying Reasons for Your Antagonism Toward Your Child. It's hardly surprising, given the gene pool, that one of your children may remind you a great deal of the other parent. It is also possible that this other parent may be a person you dislike, perhaps intensely. In that case, if you find yourself snapping at one child and nitpicking about inconsequential matters, take a hard look at the situation. You may hate to see yourself behaving with hostility toward your own child for such an "unfair" reason, but you must be honest with yourself about this. Therapist Phyllis Diamond, who frequently works with separating spouses, points out, "If the feelings remain unconscious, the parent is apt to continue lashing out at the child. Once you surface the feelings," she adds, "you may continue to feel negativity, but you can stop yourself from taking it out on your child." Remind yourself that this child is her own person, not a clone of your former mate. Focus on watching her develop her unique self and take pleasure in that. Then, too, the other parent no doubt had qualities you once admired; look for these in your child as well, and enjoy these aspects of her personality.

Dealing with Your Anger

On occasion, the person misbehaving may be you. Outside events and sources of stress can play havoc with your moods and set off *your* grouchy side. Without an understanding adult to come home to, a peer with whom you can discuss the situation and vent your frustration, you remain stuck with the emotional residue. Tell the kids, in that case, when you've had a bad day or are worried about a pressing issue and it's making you cranky. You don't need to discuss what the problem is; in fact, you should spare them unnecessary anxiety. But do explain that you might not be your cheerful self for reasons that are not of their doing—or that they can fix.

Working to keep your temper under control pays off in numerous ways. Kids are learning from you, and if you slam doors and yell when you're angry, they'll slam doors and yell as well. If you call them names, they'll grow up assuming they fit the names you laid on them. They'll also assume it's acceptable to call other people names, including, someday, you. If you slap or spank, they'll figure it's okay to hit. In fact, spanking or other physical means of punishment are particularly dangerous behavior modifiers for single parents to employ. Child-development professionals point out that, rather than stopping the negative behavior, in the long run spanking ends up accentuating a battle of wills. In addition, physical punishment is demeaning to both children and parents, and it can stultify children's emerging personalities. Single parents should be extremely careful not to rely on physical punishment for another reason as well: The first slap, even on the bottom, can offer an undeniably satisfying release for a parent's frustration and anger. That sudden satisfaction makes it possible for any parent, including normally good ones, to get swept away and lose control. What may have started as a spanking can turn into a beating, and without another parent to adjudicate, the results could be tragic.

Get yourself out of the heat of battle. Don't ever leave the premises, which would feel like abandonment to children and is far too scary, but walk into another room. Drink a glass of water. Force yourself to think about something else, maybe what you're going to wear to work tomorrow. The point is to do something to stop the escalating tempo of rage, both internally and externally. If you do lose your temper, however, as every parent does now and then, apologize to the kids. Acknowledge that you behaved badly and that you are sorry about it. Your children will not see this as a sign of weakness but of strength, which indeed it is.

Finally, remember that kids learn from your desirable behavior just as surely as they do from your negative displays. Anger is a natural and healthy part of life, and sometimes kids make parents angry. You can turn angry episodes that erupt in your family into important life lessons. Once you have all calmed down, explain to your children what it was you felt—anger, frustration, perhaps being overwhelmed—and what their behavior or attitude was that triggered it. Then let them know how you want them to change that same behavior or attitude so you won't be this upset again. Review your own responses, too, to determine what caused the anger. Ask for the kids' feedback; indeed, reach for it if you have to. This kind of discussion and the give-and-take that ensues will teach the kids that it's okay to be angry, that anger is life's way of saying a change is in order, and that anger calls for communication. Your example will also help them not to be unreasonably frightened by anger—yours, theirs, or that of the many other people they will encounter throughout life. And, if your anger was misdirected, apologize to your children. Letting them know your anger was toward your boss, or another incident, helps them know you are only human, too. Then resolve not to make your children the recipients of your anger in the future.

DEVELOPING FAMILY TEAMWORK

Single-parent families run the gamut from well-oiled organization to strictly scattershot getting-it-done, with most falling somewhere in between. In developing the teamwork you want in your family, first consider your goals. You may be comfortable with a slightly haphazard but organically developing family-as-team. Or you may go for chore charts on the refrigerator. Either can be effective as long as you all recognize that each of you is a valued player. This has as much to do with how you treat each other as it does with the mutual effort it takes to keep a home in shape. In fact, more.

Getting Kids to Pitch In

How much—or how little—children should help with routine household chores in any family is an issue that generates a considerable range of opinion. Family therapist Sheila Berger speaks for many professionals when she points out that single parents tend to go to extremes in this. "Some single parents bend over backwards to ask nothing of their kids because they feel so guilty that they have deprived them of the other parent. They think the household will seem more 'normal' if the kids have no responsibilities. On the other hand, you see single parents who expect their children to take on adult roles of helping out and decision making. This is particularly true with the oldest child in the family," she adds.

While the resolution is naturally somewhere between the two extremes, Berger nevertheless acknowledges that you may have to ask a bit more of the kids because there isn't another adult around. That's okay, she explains, "as long as you don't give them responsibilities that belong to an adult. Allow them their right to play, to go through stages, to enjoy their own life. In other words, allow them their childhood."

The guidelines that follow indicate what chores children are capable of at what ages. No doubt you'll want to custom tailor your chore list, but keep in mind one further thought. Dr. Kalter advises single parents to shift chores on an ongoing basis. "You want it to be clear that the kids are helping out, not running the house. If you begin to define them as the launderer or the cook or the baby-sitter, you have given them definitions that are not for children. Filling those roles won't leave them enough time or energy to be kids," he warns.

Toddlers can help pick up their toys and return books to their proper place. Although you can't expect a meaningful contribution, they'll enjoy occasionally trying to assist you sort the wash, dust (be sure the rag has no chemicals), turn out lights as you leave a room, and help clean up spills they make.

Preschoolers can do all of that, plus "make" their beds if you use a top quilt in lieu of a sheet and blanket, carry unbreakables to the table, wash vegetables, and hang up their jackets (make it easy with lowered hooks).

Young Grade-Schoolers add to the list getting their dirty clothes into the hamper, coupon clipping, putting their clean

WHAT YOU CAN—AND CAN'T—EXPECT FROM YOUR KIDS

- **AGE-APPROPRIATE RESPONSIBILITY.** You can expect your children to take reasonably good care of their own possessions, to assist in the daily household operations, and to take responsibility for handling their schoolwork, with your supervision in the early grades. You cannot expect them to take the place of their missing parent, to assume adultlike responsibility for running even a portion of the household, or to fill in for you in determining what is and what isn't acceptable behavior.

- **BASIC CONSIDERATION.** You can expect (and in fact must demand) to be treated decently by your kids most of the time. You cannot reasonably expect, however, to have them acknowledge a debt to you. In fact, your children's taking you for granted is a sign that you're doing something right.

- **EMOTIONAL SATISFACTION.** You can expect to find strength just from the fact that you have children whom you love dearly. You cannot expect kids to be your confidantes, your equals, or your sounding boards.

- **A REFLECTION OF YOUR VALUES.** You can expect your children to absorb your own moral and ethical standards—the ones you live by, not the ones you preach. You can expect your children to challenge your beliefs, even when you have set the example you want them to follow. You cannot expect your children to live according to your principles at all times, especially during their teen years when they are busy finding their own way. But you can expect them to follow your rules, even if they disagree, while they are living with you.

clothes into their drawers, keeping their room straightened, and helping entertain younger siblings for short periods, so long as you are in their range of vision. With your help, kids this age can now start writing their own thank-you notes and invitations.

Preteens additionally can help collect grocery-list items, prepare foods that don't require cooking (and even those that do, after they've been taught microwave rules), and clear the table and rinse the dishes. Kids now are a great help in bigger chores such as cleaning out the garage or washing the car.

Teens are almost as capable as adults in that they can baby-sit, food shop, do some laundry, cook, and wash the pots and pans. But they do not have the judgment that adults have, nor should they have that kind of responsibility, however tempting it may be to give it to them.

SORTING OUT SIBLING STRUGGLES

The birth of a second child represents a dramatic shift in a traditional family. Whereas before there were two adults and one child, now adults and kids are squared off equally. In a single-parent family, you are, of course, simply outnumbered when the kids are more than one. Siblings can be wonderfully supportive of one another, especially in times of emotional crisis and when it comes to the relationship with their other parent. The down side, however, is that siblings don't get as much of your time individually, and they often become intensely competitive for your attention as the resident parent.

It's extremely important for you to spend time with each child alone on a regular basis, once a week or so. As Dr. Koch points out, "When you do things with both kids, each assumes you're really paying attention to the other, and it ends up cancelling any one-on-one rewards out." This is often tough for single parents to pull off, since the other parent isn't around to take care of the other child. You mustn't assume any spontaneous opportunities for this, because you'll seldom get them. Instead, plan the kids' extracurricular activities—lessons and sports—so that they don't overlap all the time. That way you can devote yourself to one child as the other is off toe dancing or practicing soccer (of course you never miss a game). Ideally these take place on weekends, but for those which do fall midweek, aim for a schedule that occasionally goes into the dinner hour. That way you can take one child for a snack and an intimate chat while you are en route to pick up your other child. Also take advantage of sleep-overs, birthday parties, and the like that take place at friends' homes in order to do something special with the noninvolved sibling. Make a party of your own with a video and a take-out dinner.

Sibling warfare is another matter. There's nothing fun about that. You'll find that some of the warfare decreases as you spend more individual time with each child. Children will take out their anger that they aren't getting the parental attention they need by fighting with each other. Giving them more time individually obviously helps diminish that source of anger. There are other ways as well to help the kids feel more like pals and less like rivals. In their excellent book, *Siblings without Rivalry*, authors Adele Faber and Elaine Mazlish give the following suggestions:

Don't Worry About Giving Equal Amounts; Give According to Need. When the cry of "he got more!" goes up, respond with, "Oh, are you still hungry? Finish what you have and you may have more," rather than, "I gave you exactly the same amount."

Similarly, Don't Worry About Spending Equal Time with Each Child, but Rather Spend According to Individual Need. If one child has a pressing problem or situation, take the time to address it fully. Let the other child know you will address his situation as soon as you have finished.

Don't Worry About Loving Equally. Instead, point out that you love each child uniquely for his or her unique self.

Don't Lock Your Kids into Roles. Identifying one child as the athlete and one as the brain does nothing positive for either and can be very limiting to both. Similarly, learn to identify an individual act as mean, if that's the case, but not the whole child. Saying, "I get angry when you do something mean to your brother," goes much further than saying, "Stop being such a selfish brat."

Don't Compare Your Kids to Yourself, to Them, or to Others. If someone comments on Sara's fine swimming, don't bring up that Cynthia can't even float. It detracts from both Sara's compliment and Cynthia's athletic ability. (Besides, no one was talking about Cynthia, so why were you?)

The authors further suggest that when the inevitable fighting sets in, you should: ignore the petty stuff; as the situation gets more intense, acknowledge their anger, help them verbalize the source of the conflict, and leave them to negotiate the solution; and for escalating battles, separate them to calm down so that they won't hurt each other.

An issue that crops up frequently in single-parent homes in particular is having the older child care for the younger. It's pretty difficult to get around it at times, and if the older one is baby-sitting for others outside the family now, well, why not? For an occasional evening out or a few hours on the weekend, it probably is just fine, assuming that generally the kids get along pretty well. But you must spell out the rules, warns Eleanor Berman, author of *The Cooperative Family,* in an article for *Working Mother* magazine. She reminds parents that most older kids end up sitting with all the responsibility and none of the authority. To get around this, she advises, review the rules before you leave to all the kids. Then explain clearly that each child is responsible for him or herself and that you, not the older child, will deal with any transgression when you get home.

If your kids are chronically locked in battle, however, your absence is license for war and the kids should not be left alone. Take one child with you if you can, or send him to a friend's. Berman adds that parents often ignore the complaints of children when they've been left with each other, in particular the charges lodged by the younger one. But she notes that sometimes real abuse, physical, emotional, and even sexual might be going on. Parents won't know unless they pay attention.

Avoid assigning one child the task of being the baby-sitter for a younger sibling every day after school. It puts far too much responsibility on the elder's plate, and it restricts his or her after-school activities too much. Not having your older child act as baby-sitter can be awkward, especially when your younger child turns eight or nine and wants the freedom of coming home after school. You'll have to ignore her pleas, for the most part, and arrange after-school care. (For more on child care, see Chapter 4.) Perhaps you can offset formal child care once or twice a week by having the younger child go to a friend's house where there is supervision.

If Your Parents Are Helping Out

When the living-together problems become cross-generational—you've moved in with your parents or they're helping you a great deal—a wholly different set of dynamics is at work. You may get a lot of unwanted advice that you might find hard to deflect. Your parents' stream of suggestions and criticism can result from genuinely wanting to help you do better. There is also this to consider: Sometimes parents feel compelled to comment about how they handled any particular part of child rearing as a way of reassuring themselves about the quality of their own parenting. In retrospect, they may harbor concerns about some of their actions, and they cover this (even to themselves) by criticizing others—in this case, you.

There is yet another factor to consider. Many recommended child-rearing practices have changed substantially since the last generation or two of parenting. Your mother or father might find it easier to accept differing points of view if these come from a well-respected authority. Share your favorite child-rearing books with them and ask their opinions. It may be extremely difficult to have a reasonable discussion with the people who raised you and with whom you may have a volatile history. But you do owe them the same respect that your children owe you. Remember this, though: You are no longer a child in your parents' home. Consequently, you have a right to be treated as an adult, but you also have the responsibility to act as an adult. While you can't allow yourself to be pushed around, neither can you expect your parents to take over financially or otherwise for you. Try to be neither defensive nor dismissive and to use this time to evolve a true adult-to-adult relationship with the people who raised you.

PROFESSIONAL POINT OF VIEW

NANCY SAMALIN, M.S., lecturer, parent, educator, and author of *Loving Your Child Is Not Enough* and *Love and Anger, the Parental Dilemma.*

Q. In single-parent families, there's often anger from the past. How should single parents handle themselves when past anger intrudes on their behavior today?
A. We call this "spillover" anger. The anger you didn't talk about and work through in the past is anger you play out in the present. Anger is certainly going to be there if you feel that you've been dealt a bad hand, and we all have to be allowed to express what we're feeling. When your anger from the past surfaces, for instance, when your ex has let you down, it can be difficult not to take it out on your kids. But you'll have to remind yourself that parenting is a daily thing. As far as kids are concerned, your responses to them have nothing to do with events or feelings from the past. Parenting requires you to stay with today.

Q. How can parents learn to control their feelings?
A. You can't always. There's a quote in *Love and Anger* that seems to strike a chord with most of the parents I meet: "My ability to parent is directly proportionate to the amount of sleep I've gotten." There are times when you're going to get angry—out of proportion to the crime or even when there has been no crime at all. There are times when you've had a bad day at work and anything is going to set you off. It's easier to yell at the kids than at your boss. Don't try to conceal your feelings, but work to express them appropriately by separating what you feel from what you do. If you have dumped on your children unfairly, once you've cooled off, apologize and go about restoring the good feelings. Say, "I feel really bad that I yelled at you. I was upset and you didn't deserve

it." When you're calmer, perhaps you might offer to play a game that your child likes or to pick out an activity you both enjoy.

Realize, too, that anger is often the result of some other, outside stresses, and try to find ways to reduce that stress. All parents feel overwhelmed sometimes, and feeling stressed can trigger an inappropriate anger response. Single parents, particularly, need to find support systems—friends, nonjudgmental family members, other parents in the neighborhood—with whom you can let down your hair to keep you from dumping on your kids.

Q. How can parents best reassure themselves and their kids that anger itself can be okay?
A. Sometimes the other side of love is anger, disappointment, fury. And honest anger is nothing to be afraid of. Everyone in a family needs to know that anger is not fatal. Parents get angry just like kids, and they're going to express anger no matter how much they love their kids. Kids need to have their own anger allowed as well. The goal for all of you is not to suppress anger, but to express it in ways that aren't damaging—no name calling, no hitting, no emotional or physical abuse. Kids can find parents' anger frightening because they don't yet know that you can be very angry and still love them. Parents can model for kids that you can get extremely angry and get over it. Parents can also help kids learn that their anger is at a situation, not at them, when you rephrase your angry feelings. For instance, say, "I get very angry when you leave dishes all over the house," instead of, "You make me so angry."

Q. The parent-child relationship is intensified in single-parent families. This intensifies the anger, too. Without another adult around to remind single parents to cool it, anger episodes can really escalate. What techniques do you recommend for diffusing anger-producing situations?
A. The most useful can be the "exit"—an adult time-out. If you're in a situation when you're about to lose it, when you're about to react in a way you wouldn't if you were calmer, remove yourself from the situation. Keep your child separate from your wrath. Let your child know what you are doing and why: "I'm so angry that I'm going into my room to cool off." Yes, kids will be upset. But

you're trying to control yourself so you don't make the situation worse. Anger, like hot water, cools after a while. Count to twenty, and your clenched teeth will loosen up.

Q. Single parents of siblings are always outnumbered. Do you have any tips for single parents of more than one child to help reduce sibling wars?

A. One strategy is to have a structured time alone with each child, so that kids know and can anticipate that there are certain times in every week when he or she can have you all to himself or herself. Switch off with a neighbor to ensure that you have the time each week. When you're with one child, focus on having a good time, not on brushing teeth or putting away toys. Even if it's limited time, kids need to know that the time together is important to you. Also keep in mind that one reason kids fight is to see who you'll side with, so take away that motivation. Stay out of their fights unless they are mauling each other. You can say, "You guys have a choice: You can either work out this TV problem or I'll turn it off. This is a problem that *you* have to solve." If they're fighting over whose turn it is to do a particular chore, don't get caught up in trying to determine what's fair. Just say, "By seven o'clock, the dishes need to be put away." They'll learn to work it out for themselves when you refrain from refereeing all the battles. Having a sibling helps children learn negotiating skills when they are encouraged to do so.

Q. Parents feel pretty guilty when they lose their tempers. And guilt is the last thing that single parents need any more of. Any advice for controlling the guilt?

A. Kids are smart about pushing parents' guilt buttons, but there's such a thing as appropriate guilt. Getting bogged down in guilt doesn't help, but guilt can motivate us to do better. It's the same for our kids. Most kids are not happy when parents are angry at or disappointed in them, and they may be motivated to change unacceptable behavior to avoid disapproval. Kids care how parents feel, and that's a good thing all around. Without caring about each other's feelings, we have nothing.

4

Household Management

I don't really miss having a husband," says a Nevada single mother of three. "What I really need is a wife." For this single mom and most single parents everywhere, the hardest part of single parenthood is being responsible for all the nuts and bolts of holding a family together. "I love raising my kids. I think I'm doing a pretty good job of helping them feel loved and protected. But there's only one of me, and working to pay the bills, finding the right child care, and being able to stock the pantry and fix the car is more than any one person can handle all the time," she says.

No matter how good you are at loving your children, you've also got to negotiate the rest of the world and somehow make it all work, so that you're free to concentrate on what really matters. And, most often, in order to take care of your kids, you've got to leave them for forty hours or more a week, every week, even during school vacations. Managing the household, day to day as well as for the future, requires careful planning—and a backup plan—to ensure smooth sailing.

WHO'S MINDING THE KIDS?

The need for reliable child care tops most single parents' stated list of priorities. And single parents, by and large, put their money where their mouths are. According to a 1989 Harris Survey, single parents on average, no matter what their income level, spend as much or more on child care as do the most affluent couples. While all working parents must make child care a priority, single parents need to pay particular attention to choosing child care, which is, after all, the only ongoing, day-to-day backup you have. Many, if not most, newly single parents already have a child-care situation in place, and during the first year following a death or separation, it's best if you can maintain that arrangement. Kids shouldn't lose another significant adult in their lives, if possible.

If you're making child-care arrangements for the first time, don't panic. You have a range of high-quality options. The choices—family day care (care of your children in another's home), child-care centers (run by religious organizations, the community, for-profit corporations, or employers), in-home care (nannies, au pairs, sitters, housekeepers, or relatives who watch your kids in your home and who, we now all know, should be paid "on the books" to satisfy Uncle Sam), and after-school programs for older kids. Despite the negative publicity some child care receives, each of these options can offer a reliable, loving environment, allowing both you and your children to thrive. Your goal is finding the right match for your family. Begin by reviewing the different types of care that are available and what each is likely to offer.

In-Home Care

Most child-development experts feel that infants and preverbal toddlers do best emotionally and physically (less exposure to other kids' sniffles) with loving one-on-one care, which is the province of in-home child care. An in-home person offers you the greatest flexibility, too, and is usually willing to help with the housework. Another major advantage is that an in-home person can provide care for all your kids, bringing the baby along while she picks up an older child at school, for instance. The drawbacks to in-home care are its high cost, the lack of supervision of the arrangement while you're at work, and the ever-present possibility that your sitter will leave abruptly.

If you choose in-home care, do your homework first. Be sure to check references and take the time to discuss adequately your views on child rearing. Then spend some time observing your children and their caregiver interacting, drop in unexpectedly once in a while, set aside time to talk and listen to your sitter, and work on developing mutual respect.

Family Day Care and Child-Care Centers

Well-run group family–day care homes and child-care centers and nursery schools can also meet the developmental needs of babies, providing that there are enough trained adults to allow for lots of one-on-one time between kids and caregivers and/or teachers. Older toddlers and preschoolers can thrive in a high-quality child-care center, nursery school, or in a family–day care situation. Group care has several advantages, not the least of which is its lower cost and the possibility of "scholarships" for families unable to pay the regular tuition at established facilities. Emotionally and intellectually, group care can be good for kids, too. Research shows that greater interaction among children leads to an increase in verbal and social skills and a greater sense of independence. Established centers are also more reliable than single caretakers, unlikely to call on a Monday morning with news that they've quit. Group care also provides *you* with a wider circle of potential friends.

Be sure that any center you choose is licensed by your state. (While licensing doesn't guarantee quality, it attests to certain minimum standards.) Nancy Balaban, writing in *Working Mother* magazine, points out the essential qualities shared by high-quality centers:

- Affection abounds in a relaxed and friendly atmosphere.
- Discipline is supportive, not punitive.
- Children are both listened to and heard.
- Play is important and spontaneous.

- The groups are small and the adults are trained.
- There's a special place for quiet time.
- Food time is fun time.
- Nap time is cozy.
- The schedule includes fresh air and exercise.
- Caregivers support parents.

"Home-Alone": The After-School Hours

Over the last decade, schools and other community organizations have grown more responsive to families' needs for after-school child care. Nevertheless, more than two million American kids between the ages of five and thirteen remain unsupervised after school, an illegal practice in many states. As an alternative to having a baby-sitter stay with your child after school, consider signing up your child for supervised after-school programs. Lessons or other activities, including school-, church-, or Y-based sports, drama, or arts programs can serve as a pleasant change of pace from school and a safe haven until you get home. If your community doesn't offer formal programs for working parents, learn how to start one by calling 1–800–252–SAFE, the toll-free number of Project Safe Home (funded by the National Home Economics Association and the Whirlpool Foundation). Trained personnel will provide free information on starting a program, training volunteers, and developing age-appropriate activities. If you live and work in the same community, perhaps you and co-worker parents can approach your employer about initiating an on-site after-school program or flextime to meet your and your child's need for peace of mind.

When kids reach the preteen and teen years, many balk at after-school supervision, and it's tempting to allow young teens more autonomy than they can handle. Being in charge of oneself, however, can have some negative effects on kids. Most likely, they'll be lonely. On their own, they're also at greater risk of displaying inappropriate behavior—from checking out the liquor cabinet to just plain overeating in front of the TV set—because they're bored or because of peer pressure.

As children get older, some *are* ready to be on their own for a few hours each week, and those who have been prepared for the responsibility and are temperamentally suited to time alone can gain in self-esteem when given the chance to demonstrate their maturity. Self-care kids need to be thoroughly aware of your rules for socializing and must be practiced in safety rules—what to do if approached by a stranger or an unsavory adult, how to escape a fire, where to find a flashlight in a power outage, and so forth. They also must know that, even though you're not physically present, you remain involved in their lives during these hours. Phone calls back and forth are essential in helping kids continue to feel connected to you.

By the teen years, kids can spend some of their after-school hours in sports, working part time, or volunteering with an organization that needs them.

WORKING WITH YOUR WORKPLACE

Perhaps, more than other workers, single parents must rely on employers for a certain level of understanding and on your work lives for a great deal of self-esteem. The workplace may offer your only ongoing contact with other adults and your main identity apart from your children. Those who work for themselves or who have reached a certain professional level within an organization may find it easier, of course, to meld the different aspects of their lives. But for those who depend on the kindness of strangers, the situation can be tough.

"If it weren't for the other parents at my daughter's nursery school, I'd be really sunk," says a New York journalist. "So often, at the end of the workday I get an assignment. I tried explaining to my editor that I have a child and no husband, but her response was that this is my problem, and the job must come first." For the greater majority of working parents, integrating your job and your home responsibilities is a major challenge, and one that you will have to take special pains to meet. Certainly, you'll need to have your child-care arrangements settled, in order to function properly at work.

Ellen Galinsky, co-founder of the Families and Work Institute, a New York–based organization that offers parents-employees and employers advice on resolving family and work conflicts, described the stress of balancing home and work lives in a *New York Times* article this way: "Sometimes," she observes, "I feel like we are assembling an airplane while we are flying it." Keeping the craft—you and your family—aloft can frazzle the nerves even when you're flying through cloudless skies. When you hit turbulence, such as when your child comes down with the chicken pox and you have no more vacation days left, you may feel like bailing out. But it is possible to develop a flight plan of sorts.

The best option, of course, is to work for a company that adheres to family-friendly policies such as parental leave, flextime, job sharing, on-site or near-site child care, and after-school care and other forms of child-care assistance. Even in the absence of these policies, however, you can try the following to tip the balance more in your favor.

Reduce Transition-Time Stress. Many if not most working parents arrive at work already exhausted from the morning hassle of packing lunches, finding missing sneakers, and organizing the kids' backpacks. These tasks are better handled the night before. Realize that everything takes longer for a child to accomplish and schedule yourselves realistically.

Enlist the Cooperation of Other Parents in Your Neighborhood. One Minneapolis mother organized a consortium of five other working parents—one for each day of the week—to cover each other for prework and after-work crises. For instance, if one mother has to work overtime unexpectedly on Tuesday, she calls the parent assigned to Tuesday to pick up her child from his or her after-school program.

Monitor Yourself at Work. Are you feeling entitled to more sympathy for your situation than your co-workers and/or employer feel is warranted? Be careful to carry your work load fully and to refrain from complaining about your stress or just appearing overwhelmed. Behaving competently and confidently will serve you better in helping you to change company policies that will benefit you and others at work.

Enlist the Cooperation of Other Parents at Your Workplace. While more and more corporations are responding in more positive ways to meeting the family needs of employees, some still need a nudge. Getting management to wake up and smell the coffee is easier if a united group of workers approach the powers that be with an armful of practical, low-cost solutions to the *mutual* problem of balancing home and work.

Know Where to Turn for Help. Being vague with your needs ("It's getting really hard to find child care") serves no one. On the other hand, being able to document universal problems and solutions and to do some of the legwork to get things started demonstrates how readily some of the most common problems can be solved. For starters:

- To learn how to help your employer set up a dependent-care account (which deducts pretax dollars from your paycheck and which you can then use solely for meeting child-care expenses, netting a substantial savings in taxes to you at no cost to your employer), call the Massachusetts Public Interest Group Education Fund at (617) 292-4800, and request *A How-to Manual for Employers and Employees on the Dependent Care Assistance Program.*
- To find local parenting resources and support programs, write to: The Family Resource Coalition, 200 South Michigan Avenue, Suite 1520, Chicago, IL 60604.
- For help in resolving family and work conflicts, call 9 to 5, the National Association of Working Women's Job Problems Hotline at (800) 522–0925.
- For help in finding ways for your employer to develop family-friendly policies, write to the Families and Work Institute, 330 Seventh Avenue, New York, NY 10001, and ask for *The Corporate Reference Guide to Work-Family Programs.*

HOME-SAFETY BASICS

Every family should abide by the Boy Scout motto, "Be prepared." Before emergencies arise, you and your children need to have a framework in which to respond to emergencies, both immediate and potential, especially because there isn't a second pair of adult hands to help out. You can avoid some emergencies completely by having on hand the necessary knowledge, equipment, and medicines.

Thinking Ahead for Emergencies

To be prepared in your house, review the following list to see in which area you need to take action. If you're unsure about certain things, such as how to shut down the electrical circuits, ask a knowledgeable neighbor or friend to demonstrate for you. Being proficient about how to operate the nuts and bolts of your home is critical if you are going to prevent emergencies or handle them effectively, should they occur.

Some items to have on hand and some steps to take include:

- Have a good pediatric guide in the house. Knowing what does and does not constitute an emergency, and what to do before calling a doctor, can save you countless hours of worry. It's also a good idea to keep a good home-repair manual handy.
- Every citizen, particularly parents, needs to learn CPR and other basic first aid. Courses are given at the Red Cross and many other locations, often for free. See if you can arrange for a course to be given at your workplace or at your child's school, at a time convenient for you and other parents.
- Have smoke detectors in your home in working order. Change the batteries in your smoke detector twice a year— each time you set the clocks ahead or back, for instance. Teach your kids fire-safety rules and have a fire-escape plan. Practice it with your children.
- Teach your children how to dial 911 or 0 in an emergency. Make sure they know their phone number and address. Also, post the phone numbers of your local poison-control center, trusted neighbors, your work number, and other numbers that may be needed.

THE MEDICINE CABINET

What to have on hand so that you won't have to run out at night to get it:

- SYRUP OF IPECAC. To be used to induce vomiting as an antidote to poisoning *only* after having checked with your local poison-control center.

- CHILDREN'S TYLENOL OR OTHER ACETA-MENOPHIN AND FEVER REDUCER. Adult strength for you.

- SINGLE DOSE OF NONLIQUID (you add water when needed) ANTIBIOTIC for bacterial infections such as earaches or strep throat. Check with your pediatrician before using it.

- A THERMOMETER, preferably digital for quicker, safer readings.

- ANTIBACTERIAL CREAM or ointment for cuts and bruises.

- A HOT-WATER BOTTLE to ease stomach aches.

- AN ICE PACK for reducing swelling (a bag of frozen vegetables works, too).

- ANTIDIARRHEAL MEDICATION.

- TWEEZERS for removing splinters, bee stingers, and deer ticks.

- A GOOD MEDICAL-EMERGENCY GUIDE such as *Take Charge of Your Child's Health,* by George Wootan, M.D., and Sarah Verney, or *Dr. Spock's Baby and Child Care,* by Benjamin Spock, M.D., and Michael B. Rothenberg, M.D. Also, take a first-aid or life-saving course.

Note: If you have young children at home, do NOT store any medicines in a cabinet they can open. Also, do not give any medications to kids without first checking with their physician and carefully reading the warning labels.

- Know how to turn off the gas, water main, and the electricity in your home.
- Ask your pediatrician for a sample size, single dose of a nonliquid antibiotic to keep on hand for nighttime-onset ear infections or other illnesses that you could start treating without having to wait until morning. Check with your doctor about the appropriateness of any medications.
- Have a regular call-in checkpoint for your school kids every day. Know the name and phone number of a few neighbors who can double-check on your kids when you can't.
- Make sure your children always know where to reach you. Make sure they have a backup person to call on, too.

THE TOOL BOX

- **EXTRA FUSES, if your home requires them.**
- **TWO SCREWDRIVERS—one regular and one phillips-head.**
- **A HAMMER.**
- **A SAW (particularly useful for getting a Christmas tree to fit into the stand).**
- **PLIERS (great for undoing stuck zippers) and WRENCH.**
- **HEAVY-DUTY TAPE (for temporary fixing of broken windows, among other uses).**
- **AN EXTENSION CORD.**
- **WASHERS, NUTS, BOLTS, AND A VARIETY OF NAILS.**
- **WOOD GLUE AND A VISE (for repairing broken furniture).**

   Every household also needs a basic sewing kit, a ladder that you're comfortable using, and, if you live in a house rather than an apartment, a rake and shovel. It's also a good idea to invest in an escape ladder, if your bedrooms are above ground level and you don't have fire escapes.

- Keep your tool box and medicine cabinet properly stocked. Always keep water, dry and canned food, a manually operated can opener, and flashlights and batteries stocked for sudden bad-weather power outages.

PLANNING YOUR FAMILY'S FINANCIAL FUTURE

So much is written about how Americans today need two salaries just to survive. While there are many important reasons for both parents in a two-parent family to be working outside the home, single parents are the proof that "survival" doesn't really require two incomes. Of course, all parents—married or single—want more than mere survival for themselves and their children.

"All I know is that we lived on a pretty tight budget when we were married," says one North Carolina single mother of two preteens. "Now we live on about half of that. Looking back, I don't know why we weren't living much better back then." Unable to increase her income, this mom, like many, many single parents, put a lot of energy into cutting costs as a means of staying afloat. "I really wanted to hold onto the house, so that became my focus. I rented out the garage first. Then, with a lot of mixed feelings, I took in a boarder—an older woman who wanted to stay in the neighborhood but couldn't keep up *her* house. I became a whiz at maintenance, doing a lot of the work we used to pay other people to do. It's working out okay—certainly a lot better than my nightmares would have had me believe."

Whatever means you find to hold your family together financially will take some trial and error to work out. But you will work it out, provided that you spend less energy on worrying about the future and more on planning for it.

Finances: Getting a Fix on Where You Stand

Becoming a single parent changes your financial picture. If you've inherited or reached a settlement for a lump sum of money, and if you're something other than a terrific money manager, it's a good idea to get professional advice about investing, saving, and spending. Single parenthood brings with it additional expenses, primarily for child care and home maintenance. Even if your income remains steady, you'll have to reduce other expenses.

If you are concerned that money is about to become or has already become a real problem, your first priority is to assure yourself and your kids that you are taking care of business and of them. It may be painful to accept that your financial footing is so shaky, especially if your current life-style is significantly more frugal than it had been at another point in your life. But neither you nor your children need to be forever negatively affected by a reduced—even greatly reduced—income. Before you can act on any changes that are occurring, you need to know just where you stand. Make a list of your total assets, monthly income, and expenses to get a starting-point picture of your financial situation. (See the worksheets that follow.)

ASSETS

Suggestion: Check for hidden assets. Did your former spouse earn a pension from a former employer to which you may be entitled? Did he or she open any bank accounts or purchase insurance which may belong jointly or wholly to you? Check old bank stubs to find out if premiums had been paid. Get in touch with current and any previous state's banking and insurance commissions for both you and your former spouse to find out if you are entitled to additional assets.

Real Estate

Current market value   _____

Remaining mortgage   _____

Your equity (value minus   _____
mortgage times your share)

Cash and Securities

Savings account(s)   _____

Checking account(s)   _____

Certificates of deposit   _____

Stocks and bonds _____

Vested pension funds _____

IRA's/Keogh accounts _____

Life insurance cash value _____

Trusts _____

Other Property

Your equity in your former _____
spouse's business/pension

Vehicle(s) _____

Home furnishings _____

Major appliances _____

Jewelry _____

Family heirlooms/artwork _____

Other: _____

MONTHLY INCOME

Suggestion: Until you have had some experience receiving court-ordered support payments in full and on time, it's best not to consider this income in your monthly budget.

Salary _____

Interest and dividends _____

Social Security payment to _____
you and minor child of
deceased parent

Court-ordered spousal _____
maintenance

Court-ordered child-support _____

Government aid to _____
dependent children

Food stamps and other
subsidies   _____

Trust-fund distribution   _____

Other: _____

MONTHLY EXPENSES

Suggestion: Review your checkbook stubs and bank and credit-card statements for the last year to assess accurately what you're spending each month.

Savings   _____

Rent/mortgage   _____

Child care   _____

School and camp tuition   _____

Food   _____

Clothing and cleaning   _____

Utilities   _____

Car payment   _____

Gasoline and tolls   _____

Other transportation   _____

Insurance:

    Health   _____

    Life   _____

    Home-owner's   _____

    Car   _____

Out-of-pocket medical   _____

Entertainment   _____

Other: _____

Once you assess your current financial status, you're in a better position to take charge of your financial security and your children's future. If your financial situation looks bleak, don't despair. There are a number of steps you can take to improve it. First and foremost, if you're not already a whiz at finances, you've got to learn the basics of money management. Bankers and trusted friends can help you learn the basics of balancing the budget as well as the finer points of investing and increasing your worth.

Taking Care of the Essentials

There are two good reasons to learn to rethink financial security beyond this month's bills and toward long-term financial security. Planning ahead will indeed have a positive effect on your future assets. Perhaps equally important is that planning for a secure future helps you to get beyond any insecure (even panicky) feelings you may now have. What steps should you take now?

Purchase Adequate Medical Insurance. Until the promised reforms have taken place, it's up to you to make sure that you and your children have the medical-insurance coverage you need. If you're divorced, your ex-spouse may be able to continue covering your children on his or her policy. Find out if you or your kids qualify for government-sponsored medical programs. If you purchase your coverage individually, ask for the highest deductible you feel you can manage.

Get a Long-Term Disability Policy. Short-term disability—a guarantee of six-weeks' paid salary during illness or disability—is a government-mandated employee benefit. To ensure that you and your family are covered in the event of a longer-term inability to work, you'll need an additional policy, which financial planners say should cover seventy percent of your income.

Save. Your goal is to have three months' living expenses in readily available funds. (If you're self-employed, the goal should be six months' expenses.) Set up a schedule for meeting the goal and stick to it. If, for example, you need three thousand dollars per month for basic living expenses, you need to save three hundred dollars per month for thirty months to reach your goal of nine thousand dollars in savings. Letting reality intrude for a moment, savings of such proportions are out of the realm of many single moms and dads. The bottom line is that there must be *something* put away for that proverbial rainy day. Saving adequately may have to wait, but as soon as possible, make it a priority.

Give Yourself a Raise. Increase the number of dependents on your tax withholding forms at work to reflect your status as "single head of household." This will result in an immediate increase in your take-home pay.

Reduce Your Debt. Pay off credit cards and other non–tax-deductible bills as soon as you can. And in the future, use credit cards for emergencies only. Keep abreast of current interest rates and refinance loans, including mortgages, whenever you're able to get a better deal.

Establish Credit. Though you don't want to live on borrowed money, it's important that you be able to borrow, if need be. The best source of loans is a home-equity loan, which carries tax-deductible interest. (Separated spouses who mutually own a house will need the other's approval.) Non–home owners can get a line of credit from your bank. Establish credit in your own name. Divorced persons *must,* by writing to any and all creditors with whom you have had a joint account, inform creditors that you are no longer responsible for your ex's debts.

Purchase Adequate Life Insurance. Term life insurance, especially in states in which it is sold through banking institutions, is a relatively low-cost method of securing your children's financial future, and is purchased for a fixed period of time. *Whole* life, though more costly for the same amount of coverage, provides a tax-sheltered savings plan and is one means of saving for your children's college educations or your own retirement. If you are counting on your ex to continue to provide child support, do your best to see that he or she is covered by a life-insurance policy that names your children as beneficiaries.

Prepare a Living Will. What are your wishes if you should become incapacitated for a time? Who should make decisions affecting your medical treatments, your children's living arrangements, and so forth? A living will allows you to spell out your preferences.

Prepare a Will. In the event of your death, with whom would your children live? How would your assets be divided? Having a will is essential if you don't want the courts to make decisions for you. An attorney can draw up a document, you can purchase a simple document to fill in at specialty stationery stores, or you can receive a free kit on estate planning and drawing up your own will by writing to CARE, Planned Giving, 660 First Avenue, New York, NY 10016, or by calling (800) 521–2273.

Creative Cost-Reducing Strategies

Cutting costs, while often painful or at the very least annoying, is one way to compensate for not having a second paycheck or a heftier one of your own. It takes a bit of creativity and a lot of willingness to accept change as a natural part of life in order to cut corners without feeling too deprived. As unemotionally as possible, look at where you can cut back. Some strategies that have worked for other single parents include:

Reduce Your Housing Costs. Those who are emerging from divorce or the death of a spouse should not move in the first year or so, if you can at all avoid it. If you must move, however, try to create a new situation that bears some familiarity with your current one, such as staying in the same neighborhood or moving closer to relatives with whom you and your children have a comfortable and loving relationship. Do your best to help your children see the move as part of your plan to take care of them well, rather than as a fall from grace. "When we went from a pretty nice high-rise to a lower-cost townhouse on the edge of suburbia," says one single mom of two preschoolers, "I focused on the fact that we now had a backyard, and the kids were really enthusiastic about the move. I hated the new place, which, compared to our apartment, was a dump. But we managed. The kids will probably be teenagers before we can live the way I want to again, but in the meantime, the money I'm saving on rent is allowing us to live a normal life."

If you have the space, consider renting out a room or a garage to offset your housing costs. Good sources of renters are college students (who can also help out with occasional child care), other single parents (if you and your children can find a compatible family to integrate into shared space), and older people, who may have additional ties to your community. Of course, your first consideration is safety, so check references carefully. To judge compatibility, agree to both a set trial period and house rules at the outset. One universal tip: Maintain separate phone lines.

Reduce Child-Care Costs. If you're paying tuition at a child-care center, school, camp, or after-school program, approach the director about applying for financial aid. This is not asking for charity. Besides, maintaining useless pride can be costly for your children when they need as much continuity as possible. There is no reason to share with your children the fact that they may now be receiving aid. Also check with your employer to see if they have any child-care reimbursement or a cost-reduction policy. If your company does not offer child-care assistance, get together with other parents at work to lobby for it, particularly for dependent-care accounts, which cost the employer nothing but which can save you thousands a year. (See page 00 for more on dependent-care accounts.) Make sure, too, that you are claiming all allowable child-care expenses on your taxes, or that you file for Earned Income Credit, if you are eligible.

If you've been relying on an in-home caregiver to watch your children, see if you can find another parent who would like to have his or her children cared for along with your own by your children's sitter. Work with other parents in the neighborhood to form a formal or informal child-care co-op. Cut down on the cost of occasional sitters by trading off baby-sitting time with other parents.

Stretch Insurance Dollars. Check with your insurer about reducing premiums by increasing your deductibles on health, home, and auto policies. If your medical insurance is provided through your workplace, and if you pay all or part of the premium, discuss the various options (private versus HMO, for example) available to you. Eliminate collision, fire, and theft insurance on any vehicle that isn't really worth it. For specific information on how to save money on auto insurance, call the Insurance Information Institute's consumer helpline at (800) 942–4242.

Eat Better for Less. Clip coupons. Learn to love pasta. Avoid buying junk food and overpackaged food, which are far move expensive, ounce-for-ounce, than fresh, nutritious food. Don't shop when you're hungry or you'll buy more than you otherwise would. Buy nonperishable food in bulk. Find out if you are eligible for food stamps or if your children are eligible for free or reduced-price school lunches. If you're pregnant or if any of your children are under the age of five, find out if you're eligible for WIC (Women, Infants, and Children) supplements. Call your local government social-service agency to ascertain your eligibility.

Lower Transportation Costs. Consider refinancing your car loan. Car pooling and/or using public transportation will reduce costs, too. Is biking an option? Reduce errand running by writing grocery lists and other plans ahead of time to avoid unnecessary and redundant trips.

Shop Around for Credit. Call any credit-card issuers to request changing your current contract to one with the lowest-available interest rate. Banks will not contact you to tell you that you can change your nineteen-percent card to one that is four or more percentage points lower, but you can take advantage of lower rates by shopping around. If minimum monthly payments are standing between you and a basic necessity for your family, write to your creditors and work out a lower per-month payment schedule. Stop carrying credit cards with you. If credit-card debt is really out of hand, call the Consumer Credit Counseling Service (800–388–CCCS), which can help you work out a budget and a repayment schedule.

Cut Expenses for Clothing and Toys. The younger your children, the better able you'll be to outfit them in gently used clothing without their taking note of it. Attend school fairs, block parties, and garage sales to find some great buys. This kind of shopping is particularly good for buying necessary but hardly used items like ice skates, winter boots, party dresses, and baby snowsuits. Hold a garage sale of your own to get rid of useless, outgrown items, too.

Consider Co-Oping and Joining Cost-Saving Organizations. Join a food co-op, a baby-sitting co-op, a recycled clothing and toy co-op. Check your local newspaper and grocery-store bulletin board for services. If you and your kids frequent places like museums and the local zoo, become a member, which will be much cheaper over the long run than paying for each visit. Your local library may have memberships to community attractions that you can borrow, as you would a book.

Barter for Bargains. Trade services instead of spending or earning cash—typing for car repairs or wallpaper hanging for snow shoveling, for instance. If you rent your home, see if you can trade off landscaping or hallway cleaning for a portion of the rent. Consider bartering, too, as a means for you or your kids to take lessons or join a club. Giving time to adult friends and relatives with whom you've traditionally exchanged presents makes a great gift, too: "This coupon good for one evening of baby-sitting" or "Exchange this coupon for one car wash."

Keep Informed of Your Options. Go to the library and check out current magazines on money management.

While cutting down on expenses, try not to forego enjoyable family rituals such as renting tapes to watch together or heading out for Friday-night pizza. And make it a habit to give your home a feeling of being well-stocked—filled fruit bowls, for instance—avoid any feeling of deprivation among your family.

If you and your family must adjust to living on less for the time being, expect to feel angry and depressed some of the time. It can become difficult to keep your real values in mind—knowing that you aren't what you wear or where you vacation and that your children are your greatest treasure. It helps to end each day by congratulating yourself for doing as well as you're doing, rather than berating yourself for not being able to supply your family with all the material things you may want for them.

What Do Kids Need to Know about Money?

As for involving your children in your family's money matters, realize that they shouldn't be kept completely in the dark. Nor should they be involved in every aspect of the family's finances. Be clear to them that things may be tight for awhile, if that's the case. If belt tightening is the result of their other parent's failure to meet his or her obligations, keep that information to yourself. Let them know that they can help by cutting down on unnecessary expenses. Assure them that you will continue to take care of them. More important, though, remind them that you're happy to have them around, even if they are pestering you for some cold cash. If they're feeling deprived, work with them toward finding a way to supply them with something important to them. They may not be able to wear all the latest styles or have all the toys they want (no child does), but they need to feel equal to their friends as much as possible. Never let them think that they're a burden on you. Just remember, whatever money problems you have now will pass. But the values and attitudes about money—and life in general—that you teach your children now will last much longer. (For more information on kids and money, see page 00.)

By maintaining an incredibly upbeat attitude, one single father who has custody of his daughter managed to live through every parent's nightmare. Newly jobless and homeless, he pitched a tent one summer in a state park. "Marlena, who was four at the time, thought camping out was a great adventure; she had no idea how bleak things were. I managed to find work by the end of the summer and to rent a small apartment. We were back on track by the time school started." That was eleven years ago. He and his daughter now live in a two-family home they own. "There were times I thought we wouldn't make it," he says, "but I knew that both of us deserved a better life and that it was up to me to get it for us. To make things right, I broke some rules," he adds, "like bringing her with me to work at night, but I didn't see any other way." Marlena, whose mother left the family when she was two, says, "I was really surprised when I found out how bad things had been. What I remember most about that summer is learning to catch fish. I can't say that I ever knew we were broke."

Cutting back and making the most of what you do have is never easy. Nor does it necessarily build character. But it need not be embarrassing or debilitating; it just needs to be endured with as much humor as you can muster. It's better to think of any time of financial stress as a passing phase (which it is) and to do your best to get through it without compounding the problem with unrealistic spending or unabated sadness.

Getting Your Child Support

According to the 1990 Census, half of the five million mothers who have been awarded child support by the courts receive full payment. One-quarter receive partial payments from their ex-husbands; the rest receive nothing, giving rise to the term "deadbeat dads." Custodial fathers, however, fare no better; half of divorced moms who were ordered to pay support fail to do so.

The issue is more than an emotional one, although emotional reactions can continue an unfortunate spiral from nonpayment to noncontact. Each "side," of course, has its viewpoint: "He's not paying, so he can't see the kids." "She's not letting me see the kids, so why should I keep paying?" When parents fight this battle, the children lose not only their financial but their emotional security. As difficult as it may be, you must keep separate the issues of visitation and support. Just as no parent has the moral right to deny his or her children their material due, neither does a parent, except in extremely rare cases, have a right to deny a child contact with his or her other parent. While ensuring that your children enjoy the company of both parents, it is also essential that you receive the monetary support you need for your kids.

Fortunately, the last decade has seen an explosive growth in laws and services aimed at securing delinquent child-support payments. If your ex-spouse has not responded to your requests for timely payments, your first move should be to get an income withholding order from a judge, which requires your ex's employer to withhold support money from his or her paycheck. If your ex is self-employed, or if there's any other reason why a withholding order will not satisfy your claim, there are other avenues to pursue. Here is an up-to-date listing of sources that can help you get what your children are owed:

- For helping in tracking down delinquent parents, write to the Office of Child Support Enforcement, Family Support Administration, Aerospace Building, Fourth Floor, 370 L'Enfant Promenade S.W., Washington, DC, or call (202) 401–9373.
- For help in getting your child-support orders enforced, write to The Organization for the Enforcement of Child Support, 119 Nicodemus Road, Reistertown, MD 21136, or call (301) 833–2458. It can provide referrals to local agencies, as well as books and pamphlets that explain your rights.
- For information and mutual support, contact The Association for Enforcement of Support (ACES), a nonprofit, national support organization made up of families owed support. To connect with one of its 156 local chapters, call (800) 537–7072.
- If court orders alone have not worked, and your family is not receiving Aid to Families with Dependent Children, you can turn to private collection agencies created specifically

for garnering past-due payments. Typically, agencies charge an up-front fee of about twenty-five dollars and keep about twenty-five percent of whatever they collect. Call Children Support Services at (800) 296–KIDS or (800) 729–2445. Or to find a collection agency in your area, call the Child Support Collection Association in San Antonio, Texas, at (210) 690–2193.

Your Education and Your Financial Future

For many single parents there is a hard road ahead that, if followed, will bring them great personal reward and the promise of financial stability. That is the road leading back to school to earn a degree. Going back to school often requires sacrifice on everyone's part, but it is virtually always well worth the effort. The importance of obtaining the advanced education that will open doors professionally and financially, as well as bring you greatly enhanced self-esteem, can't be overstated. "I went back to finish my B.A. and get my teaching credentials right after I broke up with my husband," recalls a Portland, Oregon, mother: "My kids were still toddlers, and those years of meeting their constant needs and studying for hours every day were the most demanding of my life. I don't remember a single day when I wasn't tired. I didn't need to make it so grueling, but I had devoted my college days before I was married pretty much to having a good time. I wanted this school experience to be different. I was determined to do well and I did—I was on the dean's list every semester, and I graduated with a 4.0 average. This was almost fifteen years ago now, and, hard as it was on all of us, I have never regretted getting my degree and the work and time I put into it. Sure, it has made a big difference in the jobs I've been able to get, but I think what was even more important to me was how my school experience made me feel about me. The self-confidence I gained from those years will stay with me the rest of my life."

Although tuition fees have increased significantly in recent years, there are sources for scholarships and aid that can make a higher education possible for you. Massachusetts led the way for single mothers on public assistance to receive financial aid for higher education. In addition to money for school, the state will help parents out with child care. Other states have followed suit; if you are on public assistance and want to work toward your degree, check with the state public-assistance office to see if there is such a program available to you. There is a broad range of scholarships, from support earmarked by the funder for esoteric studies within a university, to corporate and government monies. Work with the bursar's office at your university or college of choice to track what scholarships may be available for you. Contact your state department of education for possible state aid. Other sources of information include *The Scholarship Book,* from the National Scholarship Research Service (call [707] 546-6777 for price and mailing information) in Santa Rosa, California, and a hot line for federal and state financial-aid information: 800–4–FED–AID (800–433–3242).

There is no getting around the fact that combining school and your children's needs won't leave you much down time. Don't try to stretch yourself in any other ways for the duration. Your social life can wait a few more years, as can any volunteer work you may be asked to do. Try to include the kids in your school life as much as you can. Perhaps you can all study together in the evenings. Mark vacations on the kitchen calendar and make plans to celebrate the time off together, even if it's just an afternoon ice skating in the park. Remind yourself—and the kids—often that the demands school puts on you will take place only over a short time in your lives, and spend some time making a wish list for things you want to do as a family once you have the good job that your education will allow you to get.

PROFESSIONAL POINT OF VIEW

LINDA BARBANEL, M.S.W., C.S.W., author of *Piggy Bank to Credit Card: Teach Your Child the Financial Facts of Life.*

Q. Single parents are often under financial pressure. Should they let their kids in on this, and, if so, how much should the kids know?

A. Kids tend to fantasize worst-case scenarios, so parents should let them know about the family's financial situation in general terms. Reassure the children, as well, that their needs will be met even if money is tight. Kids should also know how any financial change will affect them specifically; for example, does this mean no overnight camp next summer or fewer movies now?

Q. What can parents who are under financial duress do to keep their children from feeling "less than" other kids whose families are more financially stable?

A. If the kids are feeling this way, it's time to have a talk. Let the children say how they are experiencing the situation and then apply some words of reality. Point out that while others may have more money, all people have bills as well as values, and the differences from one family to another don't diminish anyone. Remember, too, that when kids are feeling deprived, it is often because there is something specific that they want. Find out what that is, and, if possible, help them come up with a working plan to get it.

Q. Should teens ever be expected to help out the family financially?

A. Under certain circumstances, it is a possibility. If it's really necessary to involve teenagers' earnings in the family's finances, discuss the situation with them to negotiate what costs they will cover. This might be personal clothing purchases or their own laundry. Teens should feel comfortable making the contribution, not that they *should* do this. Working and earning money is good for all teens, whatever their parents' finances.

Q. What can parents do to teach a healthy attitude toward money, whether the family is struggling or well off?

A. An allowance is the best tool there is to teach your kids about money. With an allowance, kids learn that we live within our means and that if our money is insufficient, we have to negotiate for more. Almost all kids overspend at first. Reassure them that this is common and that you did it yourself, but don't give them advances on their allowance. Advances can get kids into the bad habit of borrowing, which can become complicated and dangerous. Instead, encourage kids to save each week so that if they do overspend occasionally, they have resources of their own to borrow against.

Q. What about the parents who really can't afford to give their kids a regular allowance?
A. It's important for all kids to have allowances, even if the parents are hard pressed financially. Having an allowance gives kids experience in independence as well as with money. The allowance can cover some of the weekly costs that parents had been paying for directly before; plus, parents can help their children figure out ways to economize and ways to make some money on their own.

Q. Sometimes single parents really need their kids to help out around the house or for older siblings to sit for younger ones. Should parents pay their kids for these services?
A. If the parents can afford it, yes. I went so far as to pay my son, an only child, to baby-sit for himself when he was around twelve. He had to perform the responsibilities of a good sitter—getting his dinner together, cleaning up, and entertaining himself responsibly—to get paid. This way he learned a skill, and the money went to him instead of another sitter.

Q. Why is it sometimes so hard for parents to say no to children's requests, even though they realistically may not have the money for the item or event?
A. Saying no to your kids brings up the bad feelings parents had when their parents said no to them. As kids, hearing the word *no* made them angry and resentful, and they don't want their kids to have to experience the same feelings. Parents don't want to make waves, so they give in. But not saying no when you need to is a *bad*

idea. A loving parent is willing to say no. When parents can't say no, their children become entitlement kids—kids who don't know how to be resourceful, how to manage their money, or how to brainstorm about ways to make more. Entitlement kids are good only at asking.

Q. Without another adult to relieve a cash crunch, it's awfully tempting to borrow from your kids. Is that okay?
A. It happens to just about every parent on occasion, but borrowing from your children is not a good idea. If you must borrow, be sure you maintain your credibility. Be clear about when you will repay and stick with it. Don't borrow often. It makes kids feel guilty if they spend their own money for fear you may need it, and it may make them feel taken advantage of.

Q. How can parents reassure kids that, regardless of the financial situation, the children are never burdens because of their needs and expenses?
A. Make it clear that lots of people have to be careful about money, and be sure the kids understand that any money problems you have are not their fault. Give them a general picture of the family's finances and explain that the family is a team. You can all work together to be cautious about how you spend money and by planning ahead to cover future money outlays.

Q. Sometimes single parents must be out of the house working for long stretches. Is it all right to leave extra money for older kids, who no longer need sitters, to spend on videos, going to the movies, pizza, and the like?
A. This depends on how often you do it. The kids' allowances should cover a great deal of extras, such as videos and pizza. If you want to indulge them now and then, leave grocery money with a note that they can use the change for a treat. Be very careful about this—kids need time and love, and money doesn't compensate for either. When kids start to see money as love, there is never enough for them.

5

Good Times for the Family

A joyous aspect of family membership is the memory of shared pleasures. Indeed, building family memories goes far toward building the feelings about being a part of a particular family. Surely, it's the everyday stuff that glues your family together and gives each member the room to grow. But to assure that the emphasis in your single-parent family stays on the word *family,* you need to keep an eye on ways to increase the memories, in quantity and quality.

CONTINUING TO GROW AS A FAMILY

Just as you never stop being a family, you never stop growing and changing as a family. However, as you grow individually, it's only natural for family members to slide into living more separately. The children get older; they move into new phases of development. Their new development brings with it fresh challenges for you, but also new freedoms. This separateness becomes even more pronounced once the kids are old enough to come and go on their own, and some pleasures you enjoyed together begin to drop off. Whereas family members once happily got up early to go watch the Thanksgiving Day parade, even in the raw winds of November, your near-teens are now apt to forgo the family outing for the cozy pleasure of sleeping late.

While it's a great relief to discover the comfort levels possible for single-parent family living, you shouldn't let slide the importance of continuing to strengthen your family as a unit. Your efforts are increasingly rewarded by your kids' developing awareness, which enables them to take delight in what makes "our" family special. For the children, a clear sense of who they are, where they come from, and how they fit into this greater whole brings them stability they'll carry through a lifetime.

Creating a Family Culture

Many things define a family culture. The family's ethnicity, history, socioeconomic level, religion and celebrations, values, even the family sense of humor are among the parts that make the whole distinctive. A strong family culture is part of what gives children an unshakable sense of personal identity and helps them feel protected under the family's wings. Some families have a deep, far-reaching sense of family culture, which is reinforced by a larger group culture; large earthy Italian families or old-line Boston ones come immediately to mind. But it's possible for anyone to establish a strong family identity.

For single-parent children, rooting themselves in their family culture may bring special benefits. This is because they might have a need, as Sheila Berger points out, to establish or reestablish pride in their family. "Creating pride and dignity in the family proves that this family is not less than any other. For children of divorce, it also helps kids get rid of the fear that the family now isn't somehow 'as good as we used to be,' " she notes.

Creating a family culture is one of the fun parts of being a parent. To strengthen your own, try some of the following:

Surround Yourself with Photographs and Mementos of Your Extended Family. Relatives, both on your side of the family and your children's other parent, who live across the continent will seem familiar if your kids see their pictures every day. Mementos, whether the family crest, real or made up, or programs from family reunions, bring home the sense of belonging within a wide network.

Be Sure You Know or Find Out Something about Your Family's History and Members of the Family Tree. Kids love hearing about who they came from and the "olden days." Accommodating them will give you a chance to practice your storytelling skills while you strengthen your ties to the next generation of the family. Get out your old scrapbooks and let the kids pick out the aunts and uncles in their own days of youth. Make family recipes and use food to discuss your ethnicity.

Celebrate Together. Certainly, birthdays and holidays and major events such as graduations deserve communal recognition. Add to that list by celebrating less obvious but important events and accomplishments or your own chosen special day— Wednesday-night take-out dinners or Saturday bagel breakfasts, an improved report card, the completion of a project.

Learn a New Skill with Your Kids. How you play and laugh together is unique to your family too. Decide on an activity that interests you all; learning in tandem is fuel for good times now and closer ties forever. This doesn't have to be hard or expensive; if skiing is out of your budget (or interest), the kids probably won't care. Kids love badminton, ping-pong, skating, croquet, hiking, and bowling— sports that involve little or no expense. What's important to them is that you're doing something together.

Give Them Your Values. Membership in a church or synagogue makes a strong statement, but you don't need group affiliation to impart a strong set of values to your kids. The model you give your children through your actions obviously has the most impact on them, but they will also need your words. Teach them to value the qualities *you* value, not just in global terms, but personal traits such as their own tenderness and compassion. Kids are sometimes embarrassed by the empathy they experience for others, especially if it triggers their tears, and they may need your reassurance to recognize its importance. Look for opportunities to discuss such principles as honesty and integrity, as well as chances for all of you to give—time, money, or both—to charity. See if you can find a place to volunteer that will have special meaning for your kids, perhaps giving time to a children's hospital or collecting blankets for the homeless. However broke you may be, giving to others, even five dollars, will not only do some good, it will also help you feel more personally empowered. Every year, one single father in San Francisco saves all the donation requests he receives. On a night shortly before Christmas, he and the kids sift through them to find the charity they want to give to that year. "However tight things are, helping someone else reminds all of us that we are still in a position to contribute toward the well-being of others," he reports. Within your own family, emphasize that you expect the kids to show kindness and caring to you and to one another because "that's the way our family is."

Help the Kids with Gift Giving. Explain to them that gifts are a way of showing others we value them, and discuss what selections might please the recipient and why. Don't neglect the kids' other parent on gift occasions. It may be difficult for you to help out cheerfully, but your children will be grateful if you guide them to something appropriate. If they don't see much of their other parent, they may need real input, as well as money, to be able to make a good choice. Bite your tongue and be pleasant about it.

Make Time for Joy. Parenting is such a serious business that moms and dads can sometimes forget the sheer pleasure that life can offer—particularly a life with children running through it. Laugh with your kids. Play with them. Once in a while, let go of your grown-up persona and be a kid with your kids. After all, jumping into a pile of newly-raked leaves is fun for parents, too.

New and Old Rituals for Holidays and Events

Rituals are as old as humankind. They are firmly entrenched in every society because they serve purposes that run deep for people individually, as families, and as larger groups. Rituals bring five basic benefits to families, says New York psychotherapist Evan Imber-Black, Ph.D., interviewed in *Parents* magazine. These five benefits are:

- *Membership*. Be it a Bar Mitzvah, a christening, or a family Fourth of July picnic, taking part in such rituals reinforces the sense of being members of a family unit, as well as the family of humanity.
- *Healing*. In times of grief, rituals that include funerals and, in the case of Jewish people, sitting shiva, provide family members solace and a chance to have closure with the dead and to reconnect to the living.
- *Identity*. A strong sense of the family's identity is demonstrated through the ceremonies and the food, which, of course, enhances the sense of membership.
- *Belief expression*. Rituals provide a communal means to partake in beliefs that the family holds in common.
- *Celebration*. The celebrating marks this special time as apart from any other, and the manner of celebrating marks this family apart and special from any other.

How you choose to celebrate holid   s and special events is far less important than the fact that y   brate them. If you're a single parent by choice, you ma   bly traditional when it comes to celebrating holi   amily, despite the unorthodoxy of your decis   arried parent. "I went whole-hog at my   single mom, "and had a much bi   have if I'd been married. I thi   that we are family now   al was important t   ness about no   li- vorced less

t   or
                                              . Let
                                           changes,
                                        adapting to
                                      ding pleasure in
you   t dates.
E   ngs can be excruciating
if the fo   ms. It can be tempting to

make these family functions low-key, in order to avoid the anxiety they may cause, but it is worth it for the family members to persevere. Most people find that they do rise to the occasion, and everyone's presence at such life-affirming events is a tribute to the growing child's achievements.

Given that rituals are soothing and strengthening for all family members, you probably won't want to make full-scale changes in them. Nevertheless, clinging to the old ways, especially for the divorced or widowed, may prove both painful and unsuccessful. It's important to give your kids—and yourself—permission to let go of old ways and embrace new ones. "I came from a family that was steeped in Christmas traditions," reports a single mother in New York, "but the idea of holding on to them after my husband and I split up tore my heart apart. Gradually, I started doing things I had considered forbidden before, like getting together with a large group of friends and acquaintances for the holiday dinner. The kids and I have held on to a number of ways we did things before, but we've also added and changed each year. The combination of old and new seems to be keeping everyone happy." Be sure to tell the kids you are experimenting in advance; they are going to be less threatened if they understand what you are doing, and if they have input. If at all possible, keep the traditions that have the most meaning to each of you.

In the name of doing well by the kids, some more amicable ex-spouses get together to celebrate major annual holidays. While the motivation is admirable, in general it's not a good idea. In addition to the pall the underlying discomfort between the former husband and wife is apt to produce, celebrating together also fuels the fantasy all kids have that Mom and Dad will reunite. In the long run, it's preferable for you to strike out on your own and find the ways of celebrating that acknowledge your single-parent family as a fully developed unit.

Rituals and celebrations don't have to be limited to a few major days each year. The calendar is liberally sprinkled with excuses to introduce special mini-celebrations into your home: Mardi Gras night with its pancakes; the first day of spring with a living-room "picnic"; a black-and-orange dinner on Halloween; unbirthdays once a year for each family member. These and many other small (and made-up) holidays can bring sparkle to your home and make it just more fun to live in.

Make a point, too, of keeping tabs on your good times together. Tape photos of celebrations onto the fridge. Display a family bulletin board of ticket stubs and other reminders of pleasurable shared events. Talk openly to friends about your family's good times and let the kids overhear you doing it.

Vacationing Together

One of the more difficult "good-time" challenges for single parents concerns vacations. There's no question that it's good to get away. There's no question that it's good to spend time away together. The quandary is primarily the parent's. How do you have fun when there may be no other adults around? In the Professional Point of View section on the next page, travel expert Dorothy Jordon gives advice on ways to solve this problem for major vacations. In addition, there are shorter family get-aways you can plan that will be fun for everyone, including you.

Take Day Trips. Visit a nearby restoration village, a historical home, a petting zoo, or working farm for the day. Even if you can't find an adult friend to keep you company, this "trip" is only a few hours long. Plus the learning and entertainment content is an attention getter for all of you, and you'll gain the added bonus of feeling virtuous for taking the kids there.

Rent a Vacation House with Another Family. Don't think your single, no-children friends will find your kids amusing for any kind of vacation living. They won't. Instead, look for another family with whom to join forces. If you can swing one with a two-parent family, so much the better. It's another chance to expose your kids to a couple relationship and opposite-sex role models.

Consider Resort Destinations. Places where families gather—dude ranches, guest farms, ski resorts, cruises—are great destinations for single parents, offering camaraderie with other families, supervised kids' activities, and time off for you. Many family-friendly spots arrange special weeks (and offer special rates) for single-parents and their kids.

Say Yes to Weekend Invitations. Friends with a beach house, family in the next state, cousins in another city? Going off for weekend visits gives all of you a break and reinforces your emotional ties to friends and family. Most people are aware of any limitations you may have in money and space. They don't expect you to reciprocate in the same manner they might expect from two-income families, so don't let this stop you from visiting them. Take a small gift with you and be sure you are a helpful guest at cooking and clean-up time. If space is a problem for you, you can repay their hospitality by having one or two of their kids spend some time with you, instead of the whole family at once.

Travel as Lightly as Possible. It's never fun to be loaded down with all the family gear, especially when you need enough clean clothes to keep everyone going for a number of days. Try to keep what you take to a minimum, and consider shipping most of your luggage ahead to your destination and then home again if you're traveling by bus, train, or plane. For a modest fee, UPS will ship suitcases, strollers, and boxes of toys. It will save you endless amounts of exhaustion and aggravation.

The final ingredient you must all remember to bring along is your sense of humor. The adventure of traveling always involves the unexpected, as well it should. When you face the unexpected together, you can ease each other's anxiety. If one person in the family recognizes the humor in the tribulations of travel, the rest will soon be laughing, too. And then there's another "Remember when?" for all of you to share.

PROFESSIONAL POINT OF VIEW

DOROTHY JORDON, co-author (with Marjorie Adoff Cohen) of *Great Vacations with Your Kids,* founder and publisher of the monthly newsletter *Family Travel Times* (published by TWYCH, Travel with Your Children).

Q. When it comes to vacations, single parents usually look forward to time with their kids, but the thought of being the only adult around for a week is pretty daunting.
A. Single parents are alone enough as it is—you shouldn't plan a lonely vacation. Look for vacation spots that involve communal activities and communal dining, especially ones that sell weekly packages. With weekly packages, you come in with the same group of people and stay with them throughout, which gives the sense of a core family. Also check to see if scheduled activities start early in the day. That's a good sign, because it means you'll be able to get your day going right away with other people.

Q. What are mistakes single parents should avoid in planning their family vacations?
A. The first one is designing a vacation based only on your children's needs and wishes. Vacations are important for you, too, so factor in what you like when you make your plans. Single parents should also be careful not to fantasize having a big romance on the trip. If you find love, that's fabulous, but you should have a great vacation whether you do or don't.

Q. Teens and toddlers seem to be the hardest age groups to plan vacations around. What can single parents do to meet their special needs?
A. If you have very young children, find someplace that gives you as much physical assistance as possible. That is, a place with broad child-care facilities during the day and baby-sitting services at night. Even if you don't use them that much, you'll relax better knowing you have these services available. Generally, destinations that feature all-inclusive rates have the best child-care features. The problem is that they tend to be expensive. Check around to see which will fit your budget, and then go for the most comprehensive you can afford. Teenagers need two things: action and other teens. Give them those and they're happy. A number of places now have programs developed to appeal to teenagers.

Q. Is it fair, though, for young kids to spend their vacation time in a child-care center?
A. You don't have to leave your kids in a center all day. That's strictly up to you. But keep in mind that good children's programs are designed with kids in mind. They aren't simply supervisory, they have activities and entertainment that children love. Plus, kids, like adults, have a better time if they have people their age around.

Q. What are some specific suggestions that are good choices for single parents?
A. I think activity-based vacations are really good for everyone. Kids are always activity oriented, and adults usually find they have more fun when they do things. Plus, you meet a lot of people. You don't have to be physical to take part. For example, I'm very big on river trips right now—there are no phones, you interact a lot with your kids, and the river is so pleasant—but you don't have to even lift an oar if you don't want to. You only have to hold on in rough waters. Dude ranches are good choices. Ski resorts off season now have many wonderful programs. A lot of state parks have very nice lodges and facilities, as well as activities, and they're inexpensive.

Nature reserves, environmental places, the Sierra Club, the Appalachian Club, the American Wilderness Experience—these all have vacation packages for terrific outdoor experiences. Cruises are great for families. You can sometimes get pretty good rates through cruise-only travel agents. Single parents should also think about home-exchange services. Members of a service get quite clubby, and the family's contacts come with the exchange homes, so you don't have to be alone.

In general, single parents should check out the kinds of programs available at any vacation spot they are interested in and ask if many single-parent families visit there. More and more places are beginning to recognize what makes a good vacation for single-parent families as more people in the industry are becoming single parents themselves.

6

Time Out: A Life of Your Own

In the movie *This Is My Life,* actress Julie Kavner plays a single mother struggling to balance her professional and personal needs with her children's need for her attention. At one point, she observes that if kids have a choice between having Mom ecstatic in Hawaii or suicidal in the next room, they wouldn't hesitate for a moment: they'd choose Mom suicidal in the next room. That observation might reflect a little comedic license, but not much. Kids are self-centered by nature. Single-parent kids are self-centered and, as we have discussed, often almost obsessive about your availability to them. You might want a life of your own, but, frankly, my dear, your kids don't give a damn about that.

This doesn't mean you should shelve your outside interests and personal goals for the duration of the child-rearing years. Far from it. It's good for you and for your kids (however much they might dispute the point) that you have a life separate from them.

The balancing act between your own life and your role as a parent is one area in which married and single parents have little in common. You can expect to hear a multitude of "shoulds" from your married-parent friends and everybody else about how you conduct your personal life. But other single parents are generally the only ones who truly understand. While all parents face the situation of making the pieces representing the needs of everybody in the family fit together, for single parents, the puzzle is far more complex.

PURSUING YOUR OWN INTERESTS

You may be smiling to yourself now at even the thought of having your own interests. What with the job, the kids, your home, possibly school—all responsibilities that are time and energy intensive—there isn't much left over for you. Nevertheless, your responsibilities to others don't negate the importance of having and pursuing interests that are only yours; they simply mean you have to reshift your priorities a bit. As stated in Chapter 1, replenishing yourself is a priority you cannot do without.

Recovering Old Interests and Finding the New

Many parents have lost touch with the pursuits, events, and hobbies they once valued for the pleasure they brought them. You may have to struggle at first to remember what these old interests were, and to discover what new ones you might enjoy. Set aside some time every day that's for you, and review the following if you need help getting started with ideas of how to find some worthy pursuits.

Make a List of Activities and Pursuits That You Enjoyed Before You Became a Parent. It's unlikely that any of your previous pleasures will leap into view unless you sit down and give it some real thought. In the pocket notebook we discussed in Chapter 1, jot down past pleasures the minute you remember them. You may be surprised how many things you used to like to do and how many you've forgotten. "I adored snuggling into my favorite chair and spending Sunday afternoons immersed in the crossword puzzle," recalls a New York City never-married mother of one. "When Zach was a baby, doing the puzzle became impossible for me in terms of time and brain drain, and I just sort of forgot about it." This mother's interest was rekindled by a weekend guest when Zach was three. "Watching my friend pursue the clues brought back to me how much I had enjoyed puzzles. I decided then that, even without another parent around to relieve me for an afternoon, I could at least grab ten or fifteen minutes here and there throughout the week to tackle the puzzle. My goal now is to finish the puzzle before the next one hits my doorstep Sunday morning," she says in triumph.

Develop Ways to Bring Favorite Activities Home. If you're a fashion maven, scout out the magazines and catalogues that most reflect your taste. You don't have to haunt department stores and boutiques to indulge your passion for window shopping. The VCR is a major boon for single parents. Movies turn into videos so quickly now that you'll hardly miss a beat between a film's opening and your sliding its video cassette into the VCR. Once the kids are in bed, put away their Barney tapes and devote yourself to watching movies too passionate to be appropriate for kids or too intellectual to interest them. Both kinds will remind you that you're a grown-up. By all means, invite friends to join you.

Spin Off New Interests from Old Responsibilities. Since you may be housebound a lot, take a look around to see what you might enjoy doing there. Growing herbs inside allows you the pleasure of year-round gardening and benefits your cooking interests as well. Building a vegetable garden if you have a backyard is another way to have time for yourself in tandem with parenting time. One dad in Des Moines, Iowa, moved his kids into an older house, which he is methodically rebuilding. Some view that as a nightmare, but he is thrilled both with the challenge and his progress, and the kids love the adventure as well.

Stay Involved with Your Adult Friends. Your kids may turn their noses up at anything fancier than macaroni and cheese, but you don't have to relegate your French cookbooks to the back shelves. Invite your friends over for a dinner that is soul-satisfying to plan and cook, as well as adult-satisfying in its sophisticated tastes. Savor the food and the companionship.

Developing New Friendships with Other Adults

Emotional isolation is a common problem for single parents. With the exception of your co-workers, you might not interact with another adult for weeks on end. You may like your privacy and the quiet life-style that is available to single parents, but too much of either isn't good for you or your kids.

As many single parents have discovered, it isn't so easy to make new friends. The world still travels to a large extent in twos. You can gain a lot by developing friendships with couples, but other single-parent friends can offer you a special kind of sharing and kinship. Your goal, however, especially when you are just starting to reach out, should be to open up as many opportunities for friendships—whether single-parent, married-parent, or single, period—as you can.

Clearly you maximize your chances in groups. The workplace is an ideal spot to develop friendships. You're there a great deal, and you have much in common with other employees. Take a good look around and see if there are co-workers with whom you'd like to spend time outside of the workplace. If you were once active in a church or synagogue, now is a perfect time to reinvolve yourself; if you are already an attendee, consider becoming more involved on planning committees or other volunteer work. How about your college alumni organization? Most universities and colleges are extremely active in planning fund raisers and alumni events and welcome new volunteers. Should your time be limited, be honest about that, but give what time you can. You'll get back the pleasure of being on a team and regrouping with many like-minded people. Are there professional organizations you can join? These will give you access to both new people and a chance to increase your business skills and contacts. Don't overlook your children's school as another source of meeting new adults. There are a host of volunteer spots in every school. Of course, you'll probably want to check out your local chapter of

Parents Without Partners and any other single-parent groups you can find, to see which works best for you.

Self-improvement workshops and classes are another avenue to meet other adults. Many are inexpensive, sometimes free, and if a workshop fails in the new-person department, you still walk away having gained some knowledge. Check out the night courses at a local college for subjects of interest, as well as neighborhood bulletin boards. Should you find a subject that proves to be particularly intriguing to you, be it studying Mozart or Brazilian cooking, pursue it. There is nothing like shared interests to develop friendship.

When you do find someone you'd like to know better, take an active role in developing a relationship. However awkward it may feel, call your new acquaintance and suggest meeting for lunch. Or get a second ticket to a concert or the theater and offer it to the person you'd like to get to know. A Boston single mother of an eleven-year-old son buys ballet season tickets for two. "My son has no intention of going to the ballet with me," she says, laughing. "I get that other ticket to be sure I am inviting friends and would-be friends to share time with me."

Entertaining on Your Own

Even for those who thoroughly enjoy entertaining, hosting alone can be overwhelming. "I love the idea of filling my home with lots of people," says a San Diego single mother. "I'm proud of where I live, and I would get a big kick out of mixing the people from the different areas of my life. But every time I think about actually doing a party—flipping those burgers and filling the wine glasses myself—I freeze. I can't imagine being able to pull off more than a spaghetti dinner with one of my other mother friends."

Being solo does not mean you can't entertain groups and do it well. But it does require some rethinking and a careful approach. It can be a great deal of fun, including for you, if you keep in mind the following.

Invite Enough Guests. Don't have just one couple for dinner. As close as you may be to them, a threesome makes you the entertainment as well as the host/chef/bartender. Don't give a second thought to trying to create an even split of male and female. No one really cares about that anymore. But do aim for a minimum of five people. Six (including you) works even better. Remember, the more people there are, the less of your personal attention each of them needs. That frees you to have some fun, too.

Plan Your Menu So That Just about Everything Is Ready Before Your Guests Arrive. There is always some last-minute dashing about in the kitchen, but with sufficient guests in the living room, you can finish in peace, knowing they are entertaining one another. Even so, the stew that's already made and the salad that's ready to toss get rid of a whole load of host pressure. You may also find it helpful to keep a countdown card: Write down what you must do and at what time to move your dinner successfully to the table. That way you don't have to distract your attention from the guests, trying to remember what it is you're supposed to be doing.

Hire Help. The college kid next door may be delighted to serve as a bartender (make sure he or she is of age) and to help you set up, serve, and clean up. You'll get a much better rate from a neighbor than you will from a professional service. Bring in a baby-sitter for the kids and assign them to another room with the makings for their own party.

Go Potluck. Some of the most entertaining parties take place when everyone pitches in. Don't worry too much about planning the menu: A simple "bring dessert," or an entree, salad, bread, or wine is sufficient. You could also try hosting a party with another friend. Not only will there be more hands to accomplish the work, but you can mix up two groups of people for some outstanding results.

Ask a Friend to Back You Up. Why not ask another single-parent friend to serve as your host backup, stepping in to help you fill glasses and clear surfaces? In return, you can serve in the same capacity for your friend's next party. This should be someone you would be asking to the party anyway, of course. You don't want to give your friend the feeling of being a servant anymore than you would want that feeling when it's your turn.

Your Kids, Your Life, and a Few Words about Guilt

As much as your kids probably want to own you, they benefit enormously from your determination to be a whole person. In addition to the multitude of benefits children gain from watching their parents functioning well generally, seeing you enjoying life in adult terms also gives them a healthier perception of grown-up life. Much is written about how to get kids to be more responsible, but if they see you—the icon of responsibility in their lives—as little more than a drudge, how attractive can being responsible be? When the life of a grown-up appears to be one of constant work and almost no play, it's quite understandable that kids have little desire or incentive to grow up.

Much is also written about guilt and parenting. The usual advice is to overcome it and go about living your life, but it isn't that simple. Guilt can be of great assistance to you as a caring parent and can help you monitor your behavior in ways that are good for your kids.

On the other hand, guilt is a problem when it underlies bad decisions. For single parents, guilt may lead to one of two extremes, causing either overprotectiveness or neglect. The overprotective parent feels guilty in response to the fear of not being good enough or, perhaps, because of being chagrined at having an occasional flash of wanting some time off from parenthood. Consequently, he or she turns into Superparent, constantly hovering over the child, whether on the playground, at parties, or during any of the daily routines of life. This parent finds it virtually impossible to let go and allow the child to develop appropriate independence. Kids learn in part through making mistakes, but any mistake the child might make drives a guilt dagger through the overprotective parent's heart. Needless to say, this parent doesn't pursue a life outside of parenthood; the very thought of it produces too much guilt.

However, guilt also plays a role in a certain form of child neglect. It's not unusual for newly single parents, in particular, to feel an almost overwhelming need to get out of the house, have new experiences, and date as much as humanly possible. (One single mom in Connecticut, discussing her problems with her mother, was feeling somewhat despairing about men: "Oh, men," she sighed. "Screw them all." To which her mom responded, "You're certainly trying.") These parents are quick to admit they feel guilty about their frenetic social calendars and frequent absences, but they manage to use that guilt to rationalize their actions: "You can't let guilt rule your life," they explain in self-justification.

Hard though it may be to accept, remember that guilt is sometimes a friendly internal voice reminding you that you're messing up. Always listen to your guilt. Then evaluate its message. Is it warning you that it's time to tend to the business of being a parent? Is it triggering an alarm about a real problem or one in the making? You can't afford to ignore guilt, if this is the case. For your sake and especially the well-being of your kids, pay attention to your guilt and, if need be, take the action it's calling for.

But it may be that your guilt messages are being unfairly tyrannical. Your honest appraisal may tell you that you are behaving reasonably and responsibly. The task at hand, then, is to recognize that it is your guilt that is unreasonable and to act in spite of it. While your kids have the right to responsive parenting, you also have the right to a life of your own. It is just this that makes the single-parent-family puzzle so complex. In the end, you are the one who can best figure out what will make the pieces fit—without guilt.

DATING—AGAIN

Once you are a parent, it is startling how different dating is from what it was before. Dating is no longer a private adventure. There are your feelings and your date's feelings and your kids' feelings and quite possibly there are your date's kids' feelings all tagging along, as invisible but tangible chaperones.

Dating is confusing enough, and when you add getting baby-sitters and trying to make long-range plans, many single parents prefer to forget the whole thing. That's a mistake. As Louise Bates Ames of the Gessell Institute of Human Development in New Haven, Connecticut, points out, "Children should see their parent interacting with other adults and having a life. Not only will this help them realize that you are a person, too, it helps keep the relationship between parent and children from getting too intense." Another benefit of dating is that it helps your kids come to terms with the fantasy all kids have that Mom and Dad will get together again. They don't like giving up that dream, and a gradual awakening makes it easier for them to let it go.

In spite of its desirability, dating is also full of temptations and traps for the unwary single parent. Never underestimate the appeal of re-creating two-parent family life. The picture of spending Sundays together, one big happy group with the football game on in the den, the spaghetti sauce bubbling in the kitchen—it may not be sexy but it's awfully seductive. The reality is that this kind of scenario is appealing because it implies a solid, in-depth relationship—one that develops over time, not from a date or two. Attempting to create a new family by filling the void with a series of casual dates is ultimately disappointing to everyone.

Perhaps an even bigger trap is the "Look at me, I'm still attractive" game. For every parent who would just as soon forget the opposite sex forever, there are those who indiscriminately fling themselves into dating and affairs. It's usually understandable, an aftermath of a loveless marriage; but it's almost never healthy emotionally, and in the age of AIDS it's an undeniable physical risk as well.

Dating and Your Kids

While it's good for your kids to know you have a dating life, it isn't good for them to be involved in it. In the negative column, your kids are apt to view your dates as rivals for your attention, and they'll try to compete with them. In the seemingly positive column, the kids may become fond of the people you go out with. Preschoolers and kids in the early school grades are particularly quick to become attached to your dates. That would be fine, but in most cases the relationship sooner or later breaks off, which can be a painful loss for kids who may have already suffered the loss of the other parent.

The best advice for your casual dating, say child-psychology and development professionals, is to keep your kids removed from the scene. You should even go so far as to meet your dates someplace besides your home. This may seem awkward at first, but you avoid having your kids stew about every new face that appears in your life and what the implications might be for them. Frankly, you are also doing yourself a favor. Kids have amazingly creative ways of sabotaging new relationships. These acts might be consciously manipulative: A young teen, worried that her mother might pay too much attention to her date (and perhaps about her mom's success in an area the teen is just beginning to try), coyly asks her mother's new date, "Are you rich?" It might be protective: A six-year-old son, worried that his dad may be on the short end of the emotional stick, puts it to his dad's most recent girlfriend: "Is my dad your only boyfriend?" Or a child's actions might well reflect an unconscious wish—or fear—that this new person will become a permanent member of the family. A New York single mother by choice recalls the evening of her first date since before her three-year-old daughter's birth. "I was nervous about being out on a date after such a long time. When he rang the bell, before I could get to it, my daughter, who had been quietly playing in her room, ran to answer the door. I was horrified when I realized she had put on one of her favorite dress-up outfits: a wedding dress complete with bouquet and veil. I could have died from embarrassment," says her mom.

Once it's clear that you're dating someone who is going to be around for some time, you should slowly introduce him or her into your children's life. Start in the most casual fashion, perhaps by including him as a guest at a party. Occasionally begin your evenings together at your home. Let your kids become friendly in a low-key way, so that they are neither threatened nor overly excited about this new friend. Then take the kids out with you on occasion, but don't let the togetherness become too habitual. (Be wary of any date who insists on inviting your kids to come with you on all your outings. Such a person may not be able to feel comfortable alone with another adult or is inappropriately drawn to children. Whether the behavior is caused by one or the other, it should be a red flag for you.)

However carefully you integrate your kids and your new love, there is absolutely no guarantee that the relationship developing among them will go smoothly. It probably won't. Expect lots of ups and downs. Expect lots of embarrassing moments. Expect some people to break off with you because they are uncomfortable about and with your kids. "I use the way a man responds to my kids as a sort of litmus test for the guy's character and his real interest in me," says one single mother of three. "If he can recognize that their occasional demands and rude remarks reflect kids who are panicked about some guy trying to take their mom, I figure he's a smart person and a caring one. If he can't, well, it sometimes hurts for a little while, but I know we're all better off with him out of the picture."

Your Kids and Your Sex Life

No one suggests that you shouldn't have an active sex life if you wish. However, you would be hard pressed to find one professional in child- and family-related fields who suggests it's okay to have an active sex life in your home. Says Dr. Ames, "Someone in a parent's bed is a powerful symbol, and it is terribly confusing for kids." Once your children become teens, Dr. Ames notes, "You don't have a chance of restraining them from precocious sexual activity if they see you sleeping with your dates. It sets a very bad example for them," she adds with emphasis.

That leaves you in a bit of a quandary. Even if the kids are sound sleepers, there are always nightmares and thunderstorms. And kids can generally sense if there has been someone in the house. It may seem ungainly, but it's important that you restrict your sexual activity to your new partner's turf or to when the kids are away from home. If you don't have a former spouse who takes the kids some weekends, try to plan an occasional sleep-over for your kids at someone else's house.

YOUR SEX LIFE AND THE LAW

It might seem to you that your sex life is strictly private. Not so, if you are a divorced single parent. In nearly every state of the country, there have been examples of former spouses taking the other parent into court to protest dates staying overnight when the kids are at home. In at least one state, Rhode Island, the state supreme court upheld a lower court order forbidding such overnight visits. This meant for Rhode Islanders that having anyone of the opposite sex (not related) spend the night with your kids in the house was against the law.

True, no one takes such an action (or even a law) very seriously, but the reality is there. Your sex life, when it happens under the same roof as your children, could be subjected to legal scrutiny.

For many people, the question of living together becomes an issue as a relationship develops. Here there are experts on both sides of the fence. Some, such as Dr. Ames, feel strongly that it is never appropriate for a single parent to cohabit without marriage. Others take a softer stand on the matter. Deborah Matro, M.D., a New Jersey psychiatrist, says it is acceptable, "if your decision is within your value system and you feel good about it." She adds the caution, however, that this, in essence, makes you a family unit. "Your lover is now in the role of a stepparent and must be willing to take on whatever is necessary to fulfill the needs of the kids." (One caveat, however: Do not expect or allow your live-in partner to act as a disciplinarian to your children. Kids always resent having someone other than a parent tell them what to do, and they generally rebel if it does occur.)

Since most relationships that lead to love don't lead to marriage, you should be aware of the problems your kids may experience should your lover move out. You might be traumatized, the family unit is upset, and the kids may have lost a person who has become truly significant to them. For children of divorce, seeing a parent's lover move out can rival the original divorce experience in intensity of anger and loss, depending on how long and how close the live-in situation was. Of course it will be on your shoulders to handle your children's feelings with the care you had to display through the divorce aftermath. One piece of advice that can make it easier for your children: If possible, your ex-lover should stay in contact with the kids, especially if the relationship was long term and the kids liked your lover. This doesn't have to go on forever or be more than a phone call every few weeks, but it helps a lot not to have this person suddenly fall off the face of the earth in the kids' eyes.

Kids: Always Your Priority

Sometimes dating turns into an exciting rush, even after the hormonally charged teen years. There's no reason not to enjoy the fun and attention, but neither can you neglect your kids, who rightfully expect to have you around a good amount of time. Be creative in how you set up time with your dates: Meet them for lunch during the week, for a quick drink after work. Go out later in the evening, after you've sat with the kids through dinner and read them a good-night story. Certainly, dating around your children's schedule isn't as easy or as spontaneous as dating was prechildren, but there is a trade-off. Not only do the kids get sufficient attention this way, you get the bonus of being less attainable, a quality that many people find intriguing in those they date.

Be careful, too, that you're not filling your evenings at home with lengthy phone calls to your friends, examining the intricacies of your relationship. Pay close attention to your children when they are with you, even if you would rather let your thoughts dwell on the delicious night before. If your lover moves in, look at situations and conflicts from your kids' point of view as well as your lover's. If he or she moves out, look at the loss from their point of view as well as your own.

You can make your dating a pleasant experience for your kids in other ways as well. Be sure you hire baby-sitters they enjoy, in addition to ones you trust. On weekend nights, get them a video and favorite take-out food. Whatever you do, make it clear to them that they don't need to worry about you. Let them know what you are doing (within reason!) and where you'll be. Arrange a time to call them and don't miss your appointed hour. It takes only a quarter and a few minutes of your time to give them a large extra measure of security in this instance.

One other reminder about your dating life: When your kids begin to date, they will surely use you as their role model. One fourteen-year-old daughter of a single mother insists that her mom call when she's going to be out later than expected. The girl rightly reminds her mom that this is a consideration she will expect from her daughter soon.

In dating, as in all areas of your life, your kids are watching you and learning from your behavior. However they see you acting, and the attitudes they see you carrying, will become their personal measures for what is and what is not appropriate as they progress through their own lives. These years, then, offer you the chance to build the foundation of your children's strength and to create experiences for a lifetime of loving memories. The years together now are also the opportunity for you to be a powerful role model to your kids—to show them that you can make being on your own in a single-parent family a whole and gratifying way to live.

Living Happily in a Changing World

U ntil the early seventies, children of single parents were a distinct oddity. Teachers whispered about these kids who had but one parent at home, and sometimes the other students made fun. Today, schools have programs designed to support children adjusting to single-parent living, and the teachers themselves are often raising kids on their own. Coming from one-parent homes is assuredly no longer considered strange.

Much attention has been directed to the situations creating one-parent families, as it should be. But often, amidst all the concern, we forget to ask the obvious: How are these single parents and the children they rear doing? In the nineties, we have for the first time a large group of young adults raised by single parents. We can look at them and see that many of these young people are better than fine. They are strong, stable, and full of eagerness about life. They are not without problems; no person is. But there is no question that they can handle their problems, themselves, and their adult roles.

Bringing up children is a difficult job that fills a large chunk of a parent's adult life. For those who are single parents, the job has more of an edge; it's simply more intense than for those parenting in twos. It's important for all single parents to remember that not everything that goes wrong, from your son's bad attitude toward school to the six holes in your teenage daughter's ear, is because you live in a single-parent home. Every family has its problems. However, no one can deny that the responsibilities of single parents are especially demanding, and attention should be paid—by the media, by researchers, and by our communities. In the end, however, it rests squarely on single parents' shoulders to make your families work.

The first person you must care for, as we have seen, is yourself. You hold the ship together—it is your strength, courage, energy, and know-how that keeps the family on course. As a single parent, you may have to be talked into nurturing yourself. Most of you can reel off a list of needs you must meet—others' needs, which you usually put first. It's ironic, then, that it may require discipline on your part to take care of yourself; you must watch yourself regularly to be sure to be less selfless, so that, in the end and every day, you have more to give.

And your children need that giving. You're *it* for them, and it is on you they depend for nearly everything. You give them a home with structure and discipline, a place in which they learn responsibility to themselves and others. You give them a home with safety and security, a place in which they learn to feel good about themselves and others. Especially, and always, you give them love, and with your love, they learn to love themselves and others.

As single parents, you have hefty portions on this plate that life has dished up for you. Sometimes you probably feel there is more on the plate than you can possibly handle. Sometimes there is, and that is when there is special gratitude for family and friends. In the previous pages, we told of an African proverb that says, "It takes a whole village to raise a child." We could add something to that. You aren't, in fact, really alone. You have a whole village of people you love and who love you, those who reach out when you need something and who are there for you even when you don't.

It's a richly textured life that single parents lead. But if the demands are great, the promise this way of life offers is great as well. In the end, you can pat yourself on the back as you send your children into their futures with the deep satisfaction of knowing you did the parent job right. In the meantime, you can take joy in the everyday pleasures of being family, of sharing time and laughter, along with the occasional tears, fights, and making-up that define all good families. Single-parent families may not be traditional, but belonging to one can feel good forever.

Resources for Single Parents and Their Children:

SUPPORT GROUPS

● **Banana Splits,** a national group with many in-school chapters, especially designed to help children cope with divorce. For information about finding or forming a local group, check with your local school board or write to Interactive Publishing Company, Box 997, Lakeside, CA 92040 for the handbook.

● **Big Brothers/Big Sisters** can match your child to an adult volunteer to provide role-modeling and nurturance. Write to: 230 N. 13th Street, Philadelphia, PA 19107, or call (215) 567-7000.

● **Divorce Anonymous,** a support group that follows the 12-step program. Write to: 2600 Colorado Avenue, Suite 270, Santa Monica, CA 90404. Or call: (310) 998-6538.

● **Mothers Without Custody,** a national organization with local chapters; also publishes a newsletter. Write to: P.O. Box 27418, Houston, TX 77227-7418. Or call: (713) 840-1622.

● **North American Conference of Separated and Divorced Catholics,** especially for but not limited to Catholics, with groups in almost every American diocese. Write to: 80 St. Mary's Drive, Cranston, RI 02920. Or call: (401) 943-7903.

● **The Nurturing Network,** for single pregnant women who wish to give birth, this organization can provide temporary housing, counseling, and other practical help. Call (800) 866-4MOM.

● **Parents Without Partners** has over 650 local chapters and offers support to both custodial and non-custodial mothers and fathers. Write to 8807 Colesville Road, Silver Spring, MD 20910. Or call: (800) 637-7974.

- **Single Mothers by Choice,** a support group for mothers who have chosen to give birth or adopt on their own. For information about joining or starting a local chapter, write: P.O. Box 1642, Gracie Square Station, New York, NY 10028. Or call: (212) 988-0993.

- **The Stepfamily Association of America,** provides advice and information for those who are or are considering remarriage. Write to: 215 Centennial Mall South, Suite 212, Lincoln, Nebraska. Or call (800) 735-0329.

- **Unwed Parents Anonymous,** a support group based on the 12-step program. Write: P.O. Box 44556, Phoenix, AZ 85064. Or call (602) 952-1463.

BOOKS & PAMPHLETS:
for parents

- **Why Did Daddy Die?** by Linda Alderman (Pocket Books, 1989). The author, who holds an M.A. in child development and family relations, discusses her own grieving and healing experiences as a widow with two young children.

- **The Complete Guide to Choosing Child Care** by Judith Berzin (Random House). Offers insights and practical suggestions for finding the child care that's right for your family.

- **A Good Enough Parent** by Bruno Bettleheim (Vintage). A modern-day classic, this book guides parents in the art of reframing one's expectations with the reality of raising kids.

- **Your Child from One to Ten** by Peter Bowler (Acer). This book offers a solid grounding in child development.

- **Know Your Child** by Stella Chess, M.D., and Alexander Thomas, M.D. (Basic Books). One of the best sources for parents to learn to appreciate the unique qualities that form their children's personalities.

- **Siblings Without Rivalry** and **Between Brothers and Sisters** by Adele Faber and Elaine Mazlish (Avon). The best advice on easing the sibling wars.

- **Talking About Death: A Dialogue Between Parent and Child**
- **Talking About Separation and Divorce: A Dialogue Between Parent and Child** both by Rabbi Earl Grollman, D.D. (Beacon Press). One of America's most respected experts on children and grieving offers concrete and constructive advice on helping children cope with death and divorce.

- **The Working Parent Dilemma** and
- **Teaching Your Children to Be Home Alone** by Earl Grollman and Gerri Sweder (Beacon). This insightful and warmly-written book gives parents strategies for making kids feel safe and competent. Included are do-it-yourself tests for families to practice home-alone rules and procedures.

- **The Second Shift** by Arlie Hochschile with Anne Machung (Avon). Offers solutions to balancing home and work responsibilities.

- **Growing Up with Divorce,** by Neil Kalter, Ph.D. (Ballantine). An invaluable resource for parents contemplating, going through, or long-since divorced, offers insights into kids' responses to divorce and likely behaviors that follow this event.

- **The Mother's Almanac I and II** by Marguerite Kelly and Elia Parsons (Doubleday). These volumes are rich in information—much like having a wise friend on hand when you need advice.

- **The Divorce Book for Parents,** by Vicki Lansky (N.A.L.). An overview of divorce from making the decision to dating again.

- **Survival Handbook for Widows,** by Ruth Loewinsohn (AARP Books, Scott Foresman, 1984), offers practical and emotional support.

- **Living the Possible Dream: A Single Parent's Guide to College Success** by Julia Riley (Johnson Books of Boulder Colorado), offers strategies on combining working, studying, and parenting as well as information about financial aid.

- **Single Mothers by Choice,** by Jane Mattes, M.S.W. (Times Books, 1994), discusses all aspects of chosen single motherhood, from the decision to get pregnant or adopt to the ongoing joys and struggles associated with that decision.

- **Grief Relief: How to Overcome Loss and Live Again,** by Victor Parachin (Christian Board of Publications, 1990). The author, a bereavement counselor and grief therapist in the Chicago area, gently guides readers through the pain of loss.

- **Parenting on Your Own,** a series of 14 pamphlets created by the University of Illinois in conjunction with the U.S. Department of Agriculture Extension Service. To receive the set, send a check for $3.00 to Robert Hughes, University of Illinois, 115 Child-Development Lab, 1105 West Nevada, Urbana, IL 61801.

- **Going Solo,** by Jean Renvoize (Routledge & Kagan Paul, 1985), explores the issues of single mothers by choice through profiles of American and British women.

- **Loving Your Child Is Not Enough** and **Love and Anger, the Parental Dilemma** by Nancy Samalin (Penguin), offers superb, practical advice on discipline and family managment.

- **Parenting by Heart** by Dr. Ron Taffel with Melinda Blau (Addison-Wesley). Gives parents the backing they need to feel confident and authoritative in their roles as parents.

- **Teen Parenting** (Morning Glory Press), a series of books designed especially for teenage mothers and fathers. Available from the publisher by writing to 6595 San Haroldo Way, Buena Park, CA 90620 or by calling (714) 828-1998

- **Helping Children Cope with Divorce,** by Edward Teyber, Ph.D. (Lexington). Honored by *Child Magazine* as one of 1992's best books for parents.

- **Our Money, Our Selves,** by Ginita Wall (Consumers Union, 1992), offers financial advice for suddenly single women.

for kids

- **One More Time,** by Louis Baum (Mulberry Books). This story of a young boy's weekend visits with his dad is truly uplifting. For kids two to six.

- **Where Do I Belong? A Kid's Guide to Stepfamilies,** by Buff Bradley (Harper, 1982), offers sound advice to preteen kids living in stepfamilies.

- **My Kind of Family: A Book for Kids in Single-Parent Homes** and
- **The Divorce Workbook: A Guide for Kids and Families,** and **Changing Families: A Guide for Kids and Grownups,** both by David Fassler, M.D., Michele Lash, M.Ed. and Sally Ives, Ph.D. (Waterfront Books). These highly regarded books are in most libraries or can be ordered from the publisher by writing to: 98 Brookes Avenue, Burlington, VT 05401 or by calling: (800) 639-6063.

- **At Daddy's on Saturdays,** by Linda Walvoord Girard (Albert Whitman & Co.). Told from the point of view of a young girl, this book will be treasured by kids 4–10, who are coming to terms with their parents' separation.

- **Divorce,** by Angela Grunsell (Gloucester Press). This photo-essay book is designed to encourage kids and parents to talk about the issues surrounding divorce.

- **Home Alone** (Hi-Tops Video/Video Treasures) This video is not the Macauley Culkin version. Hosted by Malcolm-Jamal Warner, this 30-minute tape shows kids how to exercise safety and cope well when not being supervised by adults.

- **How It Feels When a Parent Dies** and
- **How It Feels When Parents Divorce,** both by Jill Krementz (Alfred A Knopf), for older kids and teens, these books let readers hear from other children about the pain and recovery from the trauma of a parent's death or the event of divorce. Helpful reading for parents, too.

- **Do I Have a Daddy?** by Jeanne Martin Lindsay (Morning Glory Press, revised 1991), a picture book for young children who have never known their fathers.

• **Why Are We Getting a Divorce?** by Peter Mayle (Harmony, 1988) helps kids 6–12 handle the emotions attached to parents' divorce.

• **Lifetimes** by Bryan Melloni and Robert Ingpen (Bantam). Explains the concept of death to very young readers.

• **Splitting Up,** by Kate Petty and Lisa Kopper (Gloucester Press). Explains divorce to 4–8 year-olds in simple, straightforward language.

• **Mom and Dad Don't Live Together Any More,** by Kathy Stinson (Annick Press Ltd.). For kids ages 3 to about 7, this story sensitively relates one girl's experience with divorce.

• **Families,** by Meridith Tax (Little, Brown), written for very young children, the author discusses the many configurations that can make a loving family.

• **Saying Good-bye to Daddy** by Judith Vigna (Albert Whitman). Helps children five to ten understand the trauma of a father's death.

CENTERS FOR INFORMATION:

• **The Academy of Family Mediators,** P.O. Box 10501, Eugene, OR 97440. Or call: (503) 345-1205. If you find that the battles with your ex are becoming too high pitched and too expensive to conduct through your attorneys, consider the alternative of mediation.

• **Committee for Mother & Child Rights, Inc.,** offers information to mothers regarding custody-related problems. Write to: 210 Ole Orchard Drive, Clear Brook, VA 22624. Or call: (703) 722-3652.

• **The Family Resource Coalition,** a national nonprofit group that can refer parents to local support programs on many areas of concern. Write to: 200 South Michigan Avenue, Suite 1520, Chicago, IL 60604.

• **Father Focus,** a national organization supporting the rights of fathers in child-custody concerns, provides written information and referrals for legal and emotional support. Write to: 5480 Wisconsin Avenue, Suite 226, Chevy Chase, MD 20815. Or call: (301) 589-1414.

• **Joint Custody Association,** provides kits that details how to set up joint custody. Write to: 10606 Wilkins Avenue, Los Angles, CA 90024. Or call: (310) 475-5352.

• **National Center on Women and Family Law, Inc.,** provides information about women's legal rights in matters of custody and child support. Send an SASE to: 799 Broadway, Room 402, New York, NY 10003.

● **National Organization of Single Mothers,** an information clearing house that publishes *Single Mother,* an excellent monthly newsletter. Write: P.O. Box 68, Midland, NC 28107-0068. Or call: (704) 888-KIDS.

● **NOW Legal Defence and Education Fund.** For $5.00 each, you can receive a kit of information on these topics: Divorce, Child Support, and Child Custody. Specify which kit(s) you are requesting, and write to: 99 Hudson Street, New York, NY 10013. Or call: (212) 925-6635.

● **Single Parenting Resource Center,** offers seminars and support to New York-area single parents and serves as a clearinghouse for national single-parenting information. Write to 1165 Broadway, New York, NY 10001. Or call: (212) 213–0047.

● **The Sisterhood of Black Single Mothers, Inc.,** provides educational materials for single mothers and their families. Write to: 1360 Fulton Street, Room 413, Brooklyn, NY 11216. Or call: (718) 638-0413.

Bibliography

Albert, Linda. "Coping with Kids." *Working Mother,* December 1991, p. 76.

Ames, Louise Bates, Ph.D., Baker, Sidney M., and Ilg, Frances L., M.D. *Your Ten- to Fourteen-Year-Old.* New York: Delacorte Press, 1988.

Arditti, Joyce A. "Noncustodial Fathers: An Overview of Policy and Resources." *Family Relations,* October 1990, p. 460.

Balaban, Nancy. "How to Find Loving Care." *Working Mother,* July 1991, p. 56.

Berezin, Judith, M. S. Ed. *In-Home Care.* Child Care, Inc. New York 1985.

———. *The Complete Guide to Choosing Child Care.* New York: Random House, 1990.

Berezin, Judith, M. S. Ed., and Freeman, Marger, M. A. *Family Day Care.* Child Care, Inc. New York, 1985.

Berman, Eleanor. "Should Siblings Be Sitters?" *Working Mother,* March 1991, p. 66.

Berne, Patricia, and Savary, Louis. *Building Self-Esteem in Children.* Continuum. New York, 1992.

Berrends, Polly Berrien. *Whole Child/Whole Parent* Perenial. New York, 1987.

Bettleheim, Bruno, Ph.D. *A Good Enough Parent.* New York: Vintage. 1987.

Blau, Melinda. "Divorce, Family Style." *New York Magazine,* 8 October 1990, p. 44.

———. "The New Brady Bunch." *Child,* April 1992, p. 48.

Blum, Laurie. *Free Money for Children's Medical and Dental Care.* Fireside. New York, 1992.

Borden, Marion Edelman. "Rituals Kids Can Count On." *Parenting,* May 1992, p. 155.

Brandt, Anthony. "Not Your Typical Teenage Moms." *Parenting,* April 1992, p. 95.

Brazelton, T. Berry, M.D. "After-School Orphans." *Family Circle,* 16 October 1990, p. 52.

————. "The Kids Blame Themselves for Our Divorce." *Family Circle*, 24 September 1991, p. 47.

"Breaking the Divorce Cycle." *Newsweek*, 13 January 1992, p. 48.

Brody, Jane E. "Problems of Children: A New Look At Divorce." *New York Times*, 7 June 1991.

————. "Children of Divorce: Steps to Help Can Hurt." *New York Times*, 23 July 1991.

————. "Easing the Impact of a Divorce on Children." *New York Times*, 24 July 1991.

————. "Better Discipline? Train Parents, Then Children." *New York Times*, 3 December 1991.

————. "For the Professional Mother, Rewards May Outweigh Stress." *New York Times*, 9 December 1992.

Brooks, Andree. "Between First and Second Wives, a Gulf." *New York Times*, 5 December 1991.

Budish, Armond D. "When Parents Divorce: Who Gets the Children?" *Family Circle*, 21 April 1992, p. 138.

Butler, Ann. "Dad's Raising Her." *New York Newsday*, 2 January 1993.

Cantor, Pamela. "Siblings May React Differently When Parents Divorce." *New York Newsday*, 10 August 1991.

Celis, William, III. "Colleges, Seeking More Money, Try to Broaden Restricted Scholarships." *New York Times*, 11 September 1991.

Cherlin, Andrew J. et al., "Longitudinal Studies of Effects of Divorce on Children in Great Britain and the United States." "Science," Vol. 252, pp. 1386–1389, American Association for the Advancement of Science, 7 June 1991.

Chess, Stella, and Thomas, Alexander. *Know Your Child*. New York: Basic Books, 1987.

"Child-Care Dilemma." *Time*, 22 June 1987, p. 54.

Cohen, Marjorie Adoff, and Jordon, Dorothy. *Great Vacations with Your Kids*. New York: Dutton, 1990.

Cosell, Hillary. "New Latchkey Report." *Working Mother*, November 1992, p. 122.

Dacycsyn, Amy. "22 Things You Can Get for Free." *McCalls*, February 1993, p. 82.

Danielson, Mary Beth, "Real-world Rituals," *Child*, December/January, 1992, p. 152.

Dudley, James R. "Increasing Our Understanding of Divorced Fathers Who Have Infrequent Contact with Their Children." *Family Relations*, July 1991, p. 279.

Englander, Debra Wishik. "Dollar Saving Deals." *Working Mother*, August 1992, p. 22.

————. "Cut Child Care Costs." *Working Mother*, December 1992, p. 24.

Espinoza, Galina. "Divorced with Children." *Big Apple Parents Paper*, November 1992, p. 3.

Eyre, Linda and Richard. *Teaching Your Children Values*. Fireside. New York 1993.

Faber, Adele, and Mazlish, Elaine. *How to Talk So Kids Will Listen and Listen So Kids Will Talk.* Avon. New York 1980.
———, *Siblings without Rivalry.* New York: Norton, 1987.
Family Survey II: Child Care. The Philip Morris Companies, Inc., New York, April 1989.
Furstenberg, Frank F., Jr. "Divorce and the American Family." *Annual Review Sociology, 1990.* Vol. 16, p. 379–403.
Gibson, Janet. "Raising A Toddler After Divorce." *Parents,* October 1992, p. 210.
Goldstein, Sue. *Great Buys for Your Kids.* Penguin, New York; 1991.
Goodman, Ellen. "Home Alone, Where Kids Are All Right." *New York Newsday,* 18 December 1990.
Gringlas, Marcy, and Weinraub, Marsha. *The More Things Change . . . Single Parenthood Revisited.* Paper presented to the society for Research in Child Development, Seattle, WA., April 1991.
Grollman, Earl, Ph.D. *Talking about Death: A Dialog between Parent and Child.* Beacon. Boston; revised 1991.
———. *Talking about Separation and Divorce: A Dialog between Parent and Child.* Beacon. Boston.
———, and Sweder, Gerri. *Teaching Your Children to Be Home Alone.* Lexington, New York 1992.
Grollman, Earl, Ph.D., and Sweder, Gerri. *The Working Parent Dilemma.* Beacon. Boston 1986.
Gross, Jane. "Divorced, Middle-Aged and Happy: Women, Especially, Adjust to the 90s." *New York Times,* 7 December 1992.
Hales, Diane. "Home Alone—Again." *Working Mother,* February 1992, p. 80.
———. "Letting Go of Guilt." *Working Mother,* September 1992, p. 47.
———. "Divorce School for Parents." *Working Mother,* November 1992, p. 122.
Hall, Trish. "Time On Your Hands? It May Be Increasing." *New York Times,* 3 July 1991.
Hedrick, Lucy H. *Five Days to an Organized Life.* New York: Dell, 1990.
———. *365 Ways to Save Time.* New York: Morrow, 1992.
"I Am Your Child." A publication of the Children's Home Society, 87, (Summer 1985). p.
Kalter, Neil, Ph.D. *Growing Up with Divorce.* New York: The Free Press, 1990.
Kelly, Marguerite, and Parsons, Elia. *The Mother's Almanac I and II.* New York: Doubleday, 1991, 1992.
King, Janet Spencer. "The New Dating Game." *Working Mother,* August 1990, p. 18.
———. "The Teen Years: Type T Behavior." *Family Circle,* 21 July 1992, p. 61.
King, Pamela. "Living Together: Bad for the Kids." *Psychology Today,* March 1989, p. 77.

Krementz, Jill. *How It Feels When Parents Divorce,* New York Alfred A. Knopf 1984.

Kutner, Lawrence. "When Your Child Wants to Sleep with You." *New York Times,* 7 March 1991.

———. "Telling the Children That You Are Divorcing." *New York Times,* 21 March 1991.

———. "The Person in the Middle When a Single Parent Dates." *New York Times,* 16 January 1992.

———. "Divorce and the Weekend Visit: It's Never Perfect." *New York Times,* 2 April 1992.

———. "Finding Ways to Control the Anger Children Provoke." *New York Times,* 11 June 1992.

———. "When Parents' Signals Differ On Discipline." *New York Times,* 23 July 1992.

Lague, Louise. "Holiday Magic." *Parents,* December 1990, p. 79.

Lamott, Anne. "You Gotta Believe." *Parenting,* April 1992, p. 183.

Lansky, Vicki. *Divorce Book for Parents.* N.A.L., New York 1989.

Lawson, Carol. "Toward a Family Friendly Workplace." *New York Times,* 5 December 1991.

———. "Requiring Classes in Divorce." *New York Times,* 23 January 1992.

Leight, Lynn, R.N. *Raising Sexually Healthy Children.* New York: Rawson Associates, 1988.

Leshan, Eda. *When Your Kids Drive You Crazy.* New York: St. Martins,

Levine, Karen. "Getting Kids to Help." *Parents,* p. 173.

———. "Single . . . With Children." *Parents,* December 1990, p. 73.

———. "Taking Control of Your Time." *Parents,* June 1991, p. 53.

Lear, Martha Weinman. "Shades of Loneliness: Where's Our Sympathy for Divorced Women?" *Family Circle,* 5 November 1991, p. 70.

Littell, Mary Ann. "When It's Okay to be Home Alone." *Good Housekeeping,* February 1992, p. 60.

Loomis, Christine. "Finding Live-In Care." *Parents,* November 1991, p. 287.

Marks, Jane. "We Have a Problem." *Parents,* February 1991, p. 60.

———. "We Have a Problem." *Parents,* November 1991, p. 70.

Mohler, Mary, and Rosen, Margery D. "Broken Ties: Five Ways to Help Kids Cope with Divorce." *Ladies' Home Journal,* March 1992, p. 46.

Moore, Sheila, and Frost, Roon. *The Little Boy Book.* New York: Clarkson N. Potter, 1986.

Morris, Michele. "10 Steps to Total Family Security." *Child,* May 1992, p. 56.

Nazario, Thomas. "When Your Ex Won't Pay." *Parents,* March 1991, p. 63.

Nuta, Virginia R. *Stress and the Single Parent.* National Committee for Prevention of Child Abuse, 1987.

Perrine, Stephen. "The Custody Trap." *M Inc.* October 1992, p. 63.

Rock, Andrea. "Suddenly Alone." *Ladies' Home Journal,* July 1992, p. 112.

Rosen, Margery D. "Step-by-Step Parenthood." *Ladies' Home Journal,* February 1992, p. 92.

Samalin, Nancy. *Love and Anger, the Parental Dilemma.* Penguin, New York 1991.

———. *Loving Your Child Is Not Enough.* Penguin, New York 1987.

Santiago, Chiori. "Fun in the Summertime . . . Not." *Parenting,* June/July 1992, p. 159.

Schnurnberger, Lynn. "Have My Mom Home By 10." *Parents,* February 1988, p. 112.

Secunda, Victoria. *Women and Their Fathers: The Sexual and Romantic Impact on the First Man in Your Life.* New York: Delacorte, 1992.

Seligmann, Jean, et al. "It's Not Like Mr. Mom." *Newsweek,* 14 December 1992, p. 70.

Seltzer, Judith A. "Relationships between Fathers and Children Who Live Apart: The Father's Role after Separation." *Journal of Marriage and the Family,* February 1991, p. 79.

Schulruff, Lawrence. "When a Child-Custody Tug-of-War Is on Religion." *New York Times,* 23 October 1992.

Shanok, Rebecca Shahmoon, Ph.D. "On Their Own," *Parents,* August 1992, p. 154.

Stapen, Candyce H. "Present Perfect." *Washington Post,* 15 December 1988.

Suro, Roberto. "For Women, Varied Reasons for Single Motherhood. *New York Times,* 26 May 1992.

———. "Discipline Made Easier." *McCalls,* February 1992, p. 52.

Taffel, Ron, Ph.D. "Haven't We Had This Fight Before?" *McCalls,* December 1991, p. 38.

———. "The Secret of Getting Kids to Talk." *McCalls,* December 1991, p. 42.

Taffel, Ron, Ph.D., with Blau, Milanda. *Parenting by Heart.* Reading, MA., Addison-Wesley, 1991.

Traulsen, Jane. "Where a Mother Can Help Another." *New York Times,* 1 August 1991.

Waldman, Steven. "Deadbeat Dads." *Newsweek,* 4 May 1992, p. 46.

Weinraub, Marsha. "Growing up in Single Parent Families: Effects on Child Development." Paper presented to the American Psychological Association, Washington, D.C. 23 August 1986.

Weinraub, Marsha, and Wolf, Barbara M. "Effects of Stress and Social Supports on Mother-Child Interactions in Single- and Two-Parent Families." *Child Development* 54 (1983):1297–1311.

When Parents Divorce. National Institute of Mental Health pamphlet, 1981. Washington, D.C.

Williams, Lena. "Explaining Thankfulness to the Young." *New York Times,* 28 November 1991.

Index